Acknowledgements

I am grateful to Mrs C. Bremner, Lybster, for supplying Plate 1; to Mr J.P. Campbell, Halkirk for Plates 2 to 16; and to Mrs Jo Scott, Dunbeath, for the front cover.   D.O.

A NORTHERN "OUTLOOK"

To EMMA
for her tolerance

A NORTHERN "OUTLOOK"

Donald Omand

A selection of articles from those contributed by
Donald Omand to the "Caithness Courier" and "John O'Groat
Journal" from 1975-1987

Published by:
**North of Scotland Newspapers, 42 Union Street, Wick,
Caithness, Scotland**

ISBN 1 871704 04 9

Typeset by North of Scotland Newspapers
42 Union Street, Wick, Caithness, Scotland.
Printed by Highland News Group Limited, Henderson Road,
Inverness, Scotland.

Cover: Dunbeath — Looking North from the beach below the Dunbeath Castle.
Mrs Jo Scott, Dunbeath.

Contents

As a Loon

WAR AND SCHOOL

IT was 1941. Much of civilised Europe had been crushed by the jackboot and the dark shadow of Nazism hung over Britain. It is unlikely that I was aware of these momentous happenings being far too preoccupied with a milestone in my own life — I was about to start school.

That first morning I concluded that it was not the place for me and made a bolt for it at the morning break, hoping to reach the sanctuary of the Reisgill Burn. I never made it. Two boys from the secondary department felled me in a rugby tackle and carted a reluctant, yelling pupil back to school. Subsequent attempts at freedom ended in the same dismal failure.

However, even the most unwilling scholars of that year soon adapted to the new mode of life. We were particularly fortunate in having as our first mentor Miss Sandison, a humorous, kindly and tolerant personality who was also an excellent teacher. We all admired her enormously.

What pride we had on receiving our first schoolbook, a small paperback about a boy and his dog. We all pretended that we could read it; and so it seemed but we had memorised each page like parrots and could not distinguish one word from another.

I never liked these curious little jotters divided into a diced pattern so that sums could be set out neatly; my efforts always looked like a dog's breakfast. My favourite writing medium was the slate and slate pencil.

Some pupils had their own private slates with wood frames, a cardboard box for the pencils and a container, with a sponge for cleaning the surface. Most of us made do with a slab of slate, often chipped or broken from frequent falls, and a stub of pencil which set your teeth on edge as it screeched its way over the dark blue surface.

Boys frequently got into trouble with the teacher for the unhygenic

1

methods of slate cleaning, namely a spittle and a wipe with the sleeve of a gansey!

At eleven o'clock each day was a revolting ritual when the teacher dished out a tablespoon of cod liver oil to each pupil. I was constantly surprised at the number who took it and have often wondered if these classmates have turned out fitter citizens than those of us who couldn't stomach the stuff.

Lunch consisted of a bowl of soup dished out in the school "kitchen"; the crockery was supplied but for some curious reason pupils had to bring their own spoons.

For boys keen on football the soup disappeared at remarkable speed before we dashed out with an old, patched up football to "Campbell's pitchie" . . . It was a long way removed from the playing fields of Eton, but, I suspect, infinitely more enjoyable.

THE SCHOOL BREAK

I T is morning break in a town school. Snakes of children emerge from each classroom and strike for the tuck shop where the till tinkles merrily as pupil after pupil feeds it the week-day allocation of 5ps, 10ps and £1 notes. In return he receives his quota of goodies that seem to be an essential part of school life.

The ubiquitous crisp, with its 57 varieties to suit the most way-out taste, and effervescent Coke dominate the stands. (It is a tribute to the persuasive powers of advertising that a tribe of nomads in the Sahara knew of the existence of Coca-Cola but were unaware that the 2nd World War had come and gone!)

The bell rings. Only the debris of the disposable society remains where a thousand hungry jaws have pulverised the salt and vinegar, cheese and onion, and chicken and ham flavoured crisps.

At lunch-time some of the pupils decline the warmth of the school buildings and forage for food (more crisps?) in the town. For some children the stroll down to and around town is reward enough and little sustenance seems necessary. After a listless study of shop windows they trace, at measured pace, the uphill path to school.

At four o'clock relieved pounding feet spill from the school in all directions, vanishing quickly into cars, buses and the stone canyons of the darkening town. The Chairman Mao uniform gives them a certain anonymity and group sameness.

Last week I was viewing some photographs of pupils at Lybster School, taken some 40 years ago. There were group similarities too: short back and sides haircuts — "polls" — with a fine straight "shed."

The faces in the picture were shining bright: polished and scrubbed for the occasion with that carbolic soap which adorned all our sinks.

In those times the 11 o'clock bell heralded a brief escape: a thunder of tackity boots across the playground took us to Miller's shop, where we pushed and jostled our way to the counter. And there: piping hot meat pies and jelly ones, all currants and juice. The pies cost 2d. each (less than 1p in decimal money). Back to school and woe betide you if unwashed hands settled on the spotless white paper in the art class.

Villagers dashed home for lunch, often a plateful of good homely porridge. Country bairns squatted around the cloakroom with scones, oatcakes and milk. . . I can still smell the home-made butter spread thick and yellow on their pieces.

BOYS' FOOTBALL

LAST week (June 1976) I was a spectator at a football match between Halkirk and Thurso Boys' Brigades. Many of these boys' games prove more interesting spectacles than the adult matches, so often charged with ill feeling and the strong desire to physically curb any skill in the opposition.

How well turned out are the young footballers of nowadays: fresh, clean strips (all the same colour) and stockings to match, with boots scientifically designed and embellished with white plastic strips. The Thurso boys even have their own personal transport to take them to away games.

What a contrast it was to some 25-30 years ago when we used to make our annual foray from Lybster to Dunbeath. Some players travelled by bus and others by bike, occasionally taking a passenger on the bar! Many a game we started with only nine men and two still in transit!

To the young boys of today we must have appeared hilarious with short-back-and-sides, home-produced haircuts, some obviously done with a bowlie! On occasions neither side had a football strip and confusion reigned with twenty-two players all in drab, grey shirts. Some fellows played in shorts and others with dungarees tucked into their socks.

The calibre and quality of footwear was highly variable, from soft gymshoes to leather shoes, tackity boots (usually worn by a full-back) or football boots — sometimes shared by the players. Anyone who had a poor first half might be persuaded by the team to give his boots to somebody who might prove better in the second half. It was a humiliating experience.

Few of the young boys now seem to wear shinguards. We did —
usually a paperback detective or western that worked its way out of
the too-short socks and ended up strewn on the field.

In those days we knew nothing of football theory: strikers, midfield
men and sweepers were unborn. Our tactics discussion was always
brief: "We'll jist hev till beat them, boys."

There were no managers, coaches or selection committees to
criticise us; if we lost (which often happened) we philosophised at the
shoppie that the Dunbeathers always played dirty and the ref. was on
their side anyway.

Likely they said the same about us when playing at Lybster.

SCHOOL HOLIDAYS: LYBSTER

T HE summer holidays have been received by the pupils with the
usual unbounded enthusiasm. How long six weeks
seem to a peedie boy whose mind thinks within such a short time
scale.

In retrospect the summers of childhood seem sunnier, more
cheerful and full of such varied activities compared to the holidays of
today's bairns. Likely folk have aye thought the same.

School I generally regarded as an imposition by a repressive adult
society on the natural freedom of childhood. So did my con-
temporaries, as we gazed wistfully through school windows while the
bonnie days of June edged by our concrete enclosure.

On the last day of session school prizes, one per subject, were issued
to loons and lassies. Lucky characters, born with brains! Chiels born
with big feet got nothing. The bell finally tolled and flying boots soon
emptied the school for its annual clean out.

A favoured spot in the holidays was the Ha' where trees and bushes
played host to a million birds. I can still get the heady scent of the
gorse whose yellow buds gave off such brilliance to the sun.

Perhaps a round of golf would follow. We never paid a membership,
but hacked happily around, setting our disintegrating golf balls up on
bushies for every shot. We always played preferred lies! The clubs
were normally of the variety now found in golf museums, with
hickory shafts and rusty heads. The normal complement was two of
these and a putter. One well-off fellow who sported a wood was the
subject of much envy.

Two hours of that might tempt you to Shelligoe to cool tired feet.
Some bolder fellows scampered up the big rock (a large triangular sea

stack) and basked in the sun. Close by, a burnie emptied in to the sea and in its cascades tiny eels writhed.

On catching them you exclaimed:

"Eel-iot, eel-iot, pit a knot on yer tail, An' I'll let ye back till yer own home again."

Sometimes they obliged.

Shouts at the end of the village signalled a gamey of football, played with an object held together by an assortment of crude patches from which emerged sausages of bladder that threatened to erupt at any time. The sides were gradually depleted with successive shouts of "Yer mither wants ye." Time to drift back up the village.

THE HOME GUARD

SOMETIMES the dark silence of the long winters of early boyhood were broken by the sullen boom of Scapa guns sending sonorous echoes into the night sky of Caithness. Accompanying searchlights cut the air and swept the heavens for a hidden foe. The name "Scapa Flow" had a romantic yet fearful aura; peedie boys from Lybster knew it was in Orkney, but the islands were as far beyond our ken as the homeland of the Luftwaffe.

Hitler, it seems, had concern for Scapa, ringed by booms, bristling with guns and manned by thousands of professional troops. What thoughts, I wonder, did the Fuhrer have on such worthy military part-timers as the Home Guard, in particular the Lybster and Dunbeath companies, who frequently held mock battles with each other? These encounters, of the most earnest nature, had their humorous moments.

A contingent from Lybster was attacking neighbouring Dunbeath, whose defenders had carefully concealed themselves from the moonlit sky. Beyond the Dunbeath encampment a figure stirred.

"Halt! Who goes there?"

"Kushi."

"Where are you from?"

"Pakistan."

"From Pakistan! Heavens! And John the Chemist's no here yet from Lybster!"

With some Home Guard stalwarts the authenticity of an exercise was carried to the ultimate. The Lybster company was divided into two groups, each one trying to gain access to the other's territory. An intrusive figure appeared over the brow of a hill.

"Halt! Who goes there?" No response. The challenge was repeated. Still no response as the figure advanced. "Bang! Yer deid!" The figure slumped to the ground and lay lifeless.

Two men scurried to the "lifeless" intruder and shone a torch on his face. "Oh it's yersel Jeemag. Where's the rest o' them? Come on, tell us!"

A jaundiced eye gazed up from the sodden moor and tight lips muttered: "Dead men tell no tales!"

BAGPIPES

I was rooting around in the loft last week and came across what had been a set of bagpipes: the Seaforth tartan was moth-eaten, the bag perished and the drones heavy in mould. I carefully removed the corpse and carried it gingerly into the living room where a small boy who was visiting us stopped suddenly in mid stride and said tearfully, "Does it bite?"

That very set of pipes had once marched proudly with the Lybster Boys' Brigade band which entertained a marvelling public in the village and distant parts such as Dunbeath and Helmsdale. Our first tutor was a man of considerable patience and good humour: Davie Sinclair from Occumster. His pupils skraiked their way through scales, doublings and grace notes until discerning listeners could distinguish: Highland Laddie, Dornoch Links, the 79th Farewell to Gibralter, The Earl of Mansfield, Loudon's Bonnie Woods and Braes and The High Road to Linton. Our repertoire hardly matched that of the Strathclyde police, but I'm sure we were a much bigger draw in Lybster!

How many members of the band still have a tune on the pipes, that marvellously evocative instrument of ancient lineage?

So old is its heritage that some piping historians trace its foundations to over 5000 years ago, to the prototype of a pipe played with a single reed. Until the Middle Ages, illustrations usually indicate a pipe with a single or double chanter. The introduction of a drone is thought to have taken place some 600 or 700 years ago and there is a 16th century reference in Scotland to "The drone bagpipe ..... made of ane bleddir and of ane reid".

It is thought that what we now recognise in Northern Scotland as a standard set of pipes evolved in the 18th century, with blowstick, chanter and three drones — two tenor and a bass.

No one knows when the bagpipe first arrived in the Highlands; the date of its introduction will perhaps always be lost in the mists of antiquity. Yet the Highlanders made the instrument their own, taking its stirring and melancholic notes to all the corners of the world.

THE HARVEST

L AST week the sun vanished with an abruptness that surprised us all, leaving the sky to the wild energies of a nor'-wester and the heavy pewter clouds it drove from Arctic shores. Ganseys and coats crept out of dark cupboards to face the knives and arrows of the chilling gale.

Farmers scanned the thick greyness of the sky, frowned at the scubs of rain, and looked for the shafts of silvery light that would herald the passing front.

Wind or no wind, the work in the harvest field goes on, leaving the long summer in its wake. Field after field is attacked by the combine, a voracious space-age monster, who gorges the fruits of the Caithness soil and swathes the lifeless straw on the shorn stubble. Baler follows combine, wrapping the straw into huge cylinders which perch ill at ease in the low profiles of the Caithness landscape.

The clinical efficiency of it all has transformed what was once a joyous, communal effort of one crofting neighbour with another into a factory operation.

Look at the life that was in the binder clanging and rattling its way round the golden field, offering its fulsome sheaf to the gods of the harvest! What satisfaction in setting up the stooks, heads heavy with ripeness of summer!

As bairns, running wild and free along the sharp stubble, what magic we found in the moonful harvest nights, hearing the rustle of the corn ears and hiding deep in the stooks, hearts pounding for fear of discovery during a game of hide and seek.

A week or two would have to pass before we could admire the skill of the crofters building their conical stacks. And the day of the mill was still to come.

"Donald' Allan's mill!" Away we scampered to its destination eager for the chance to carry buckets of water to the mill while threshing was in progress. On windy days chaff was everywhere, including our eyes. Previous generations will remember the chaff being carefully collected to replenish the "caff sek."

Few people nowadays wear the harvest knots that used to be so plentiful when I was a schoolboy. Some of the designs were ingenious, a tribute to the skill and patience of the maker.

Harvest queens and thanksgivings still survive but somehow the cycle nowadays is not completed. The barn is uncleared, the boxie, fiddle and pipes lie in melancholy silence; no "hoochs" ring the old rafters and the moon is cold about the alien bales in the fields.

HALLOWEEN & GUIZERS

W HAT brilliant light there was on the evening of 31st October; you could have driven without headlights. A great orb of moon glistened from the purple canopy of heaven and played its delicate beams on the patterned waves of the sea. Moonlight on water is Nature's greatest therapy.

Far beyond the strong granite brow of the Ord a necklace of sparkling lights was strung from the sea to the stars. Even oilrigs can look beautiful!

What an evening for the Caithness autumn to take its exit: a giant moon riding high in the sky, rugged, tinted cliffs, ghostly sea stacks and the broad sweep of the dark hills away to lost horizons. An ideal night for warlocks and witches and things that go bump in the night. Glad am I to be so far distant from Kirk Alloway and the fiends who terrified Tam O'Shanter!

The standing stone at Latheron looms up in the cold light. What mischief will the people of the other world play around it and among the rock pillars of Achavanich or Guidebest tonight? Such places exude power at this time of year and stones are known to stalk silently and bathe in the nearest water on Hallowe'en.

It has long been considered unlucky to move a standing stone and many a farmer has suffered loss of his animals following such an act of desecration. One foolhardy fellow near Guidebest attempted to remove a stone. Next day, a horse died. Undeterred, he renewed his efforts to have the stone displaced and his mother-in-law died. The tragedies that befell the remover of an entire stone circle in Latheron Parish are not recorded!

The last of the Guizers straggle along the streets of Halkirk village. It is difficult to tell who they are nowadays with these horrendous masks reminiscent of Planet of the Apes.

Maybe it was just as difficult to recognise the Guizers of 40 years ago: loons in old boots, baggy breeks, tattered jackets, nylon stocking mask and outsize cap.

Few of us did any acts for the apples, nuts or pennies received. Perhaps we were untalented, too shy or too mercenary and eager to be off to the next house.

Many a tongue wagging was dished out to us by wifies in peenies. "Now don't be up to devilment" was their common warning. I suppose, like other good advice given, it went unheeded.

I get out of the car and shiver in the chilly air. An eerie, scowling face glows through the gaunt leafless trees of Braal. It might be a neepie lantern. On the other hand it might be a ... The house door slams shut sending lingering echoes along the unknown corridors of the night.

AUTUMN

S UMMER took a dramatic leap into autumn last week and appears to have every intention of staying there, gathering up cold Icelandic winds and throwing them unimpeded on to the vulnerable lowlands of Caithness.

Autumn in Caithness! Scarcely mellow but with some fruitfulness.

I am thinking particularly of boyhood in Lybster in late September when we worked our way along the ravine of the Reisgill burn collecting hazel nuts. Usually they were picked green as we could not wait for the full growth of the kernel in its polished mahogany husk. The nuts were seldom carried home, but cracked by eager teeth and devoured by hungry mouths. What risks we took crawling higher among the slender branches to reach a seductive cluster of the nuts. On one occasion a branch gave way beneath my weight and I tumbled through the foliage to be caught by the dungaree braces and left suspended in space before being rescued. Some weeks earlier a crony of mine had fallen 100 feet over the cliffs and ended up with a broken toe! His incredible escape made the front page of the national press.

What a dare-devil he was! On one occasion we raced each other for a six pence across the parapet of the Reisgill Bridge by the harbour, oblivious of the 60 foot drop below. His most amazing stunt was to leap with a homemade parachute from a bedroom window. The 'chute failed to open and "operation paratroop" was abandoned!

His agility and daring was much admired on these nut-picking escapades. At the foot of every tree he scaled would gather a gaggle of boys eagerly awaiting the harvest that tumbled to the ground.

A good year for the nuts and a good harvest often went together. A double nut in a kernel was uncommon and considered lucky. I have even heard it said that carrying it in your pocket was a certain cure against toothache.

Down in south-west England a rich harvest of hazel nuts was believed to foretell many deaths. Another old wives' tale relates how dangerous it was to go nutting on a Sunday as the Devil might put you in his bag. We didn't go on the Sabbath for other reasons, not least of them the prospect of a well-delivered luggard!

WINTER

IN a recent news broadcast the BBC announced that a number of roads in North Britain (Yorkshire) were blocked. No mention was made of the fact that the two roads down to Braal, Halkirk, were quite impassable until a friendly JCB excavator gorged its way through the drifts in which delighted children had cut snow houses.

Our youngsters have grown so used to mild winters that they relished plowtering about in the deep, soft snow.

The blocked road reminded me of the 1947 winter when snow drifted for days on end, blocking many country roads and village ones forbye. What a joyous time it was! Days on end off school! Huge snowhouses and snowmen built in the middle of Lybster's main street!

To crown it all a snow plough, with lorry heaped high in sand, charged at the drifts in the village, sending out great spumes of snow. But only for a few dozen yards. It too became completely locked in the white fastness — and extended our school holiday.

We had no thick padded anoraks then. A few old "ganseys" sufficed with a cast-off or handed-down jacket on top. Balaclavas were worn hauled down over the loogs to keep them warm or rolled up in such a way that they resembled a skullcap. As nearly all young boys wore short trousers, dungarees were added in winter.

The most prized possession in times of snow and ice was the pair of tackety boots, with rows of gleaming studs, a steel toe-shod and heel-shod protecting the extremities of the foot. They were magnificent on ice!

Beside our school was a flat concrete foundation, all that was left of a war-time shelter. It was an ideal base on which to make slides, which had a much finer and faster finish if you first slooshed them with water and allowed them to freeze hard before sliding.

The main sledge runs were the Shore Road and Jock's Brae. In suitable conditions sledgers could set off from near the Bay View Hotel and career at increasing speed down to the harbour. A sledge run of nearly a mile! But what a long trek back to the starting grid.

The sledge journey could be a hazardous one, the occasional driver and his vehicle leaving the run to cavort down the steep brae leading to the Inner Basin. Fishing boats, tied up at the harbour, on at least two occasions, prevented sledgers landing in the drink.

I have clearer recollections of the winter evening scenes on Jock's Brae, where dozens of bemuffled sledgers collected on crisp, starlit evenings. Some of the sledges were huge and could seat four comfortably, the driver at the front spraying up snow as he dug his heel-shods into the packed snow in order to steer.

The fastest run was obtained by pushing the sledge in front and then doing a belly-flopper on to it, steering with the hard toes of the boots.... No lure of a winter holiday in some fashionable Continental resort could have dragged me away from it.

JANUARY

WHEN I was a loon in Lybster a standard item on the New Year's menu was a duff, liberally peppered with half-pennies, threepenny and sixpenny pieces. Inserted with them was a white button which bachelors hoped to avoid as it was regarded as a portent of continuing bachelordom. For a week or so the diminishing duff would survive to be eaten cold with milk or fried with butter. Either way it was delicious and an excellent filler of the bottomless pit that served young boys as a stomach!

Stomachs have taken the most savage treatment over the past ten days and could do with a civilised diet of brose and tatties and herring over the next month.

At least some of our feathered friends are dining à la carte at the moment on the rich scrapings from the festive plate. One of our two resident robins has been so preoccupied chasing away the sparrows that he has had little time to set his digestive juices to work. His territorial problems have been aggravated by the other robin who makes the most audacious commando raids on the jealously guarded terrain.

The clusters of starlings seem noisier than ever; maybe the idiocies of Westminster discussion are transferred to them when Parliament goes in to recess!

Perhaps I do the starlings an injustice. It could be that our colony of rooks (numbering 635) has donned Parliament's mantle, considering the unholy noise they make as dusk steals quietly down the valley.

A warm snap of weather in January could well lead to unseasonal amorous advances among the birds, even the male rooks, who sit high in the skeletal branches of the wood and proclaim their ecstatic joy in the most unmelodious way.

The weather can fool the rooks and forecasters. A glance at a weather chart last week showed thunder was imminent. "Is no thunder in January a bad omen for the coming spring?" queried a neighbour. The thunder failed to appear and so all might still be well with lambs and crops.

Most of us have a primitive fear of thunder: an awesome regard for Nature's unleashed power; and dimly remembered warnings of the wrath of a vengeful God; or merely Thor on one of his chauvinistic charges across the heavens.

FEBRUARY

T HE ice-cold winds that have howled in from the north during and since the festive season have on no occasion led me to agree with people saying: "What terrible weather!"

On the contrary, I have welcomed the chilly blasts and carpet of snow: instead of the irksome labour of breaking in a new garden I can, in all conscience, nestle into an armchair and take up the less onerous task of reading books.

During the past fortnight I have re-read three of Neil Gunn's novels, whose delightful prose portrays community life of the Highland crofter/fishermen. I am sure that I would have been much more interested in literature at school had these been the set books rather than the long-winded novels of Sir Walter Scott that were deemed desirable for my education. It scunnered me of Scott then and the distaste survives.

Neil Gunn's knowledge of the sea and fishermen was gleaned from his own personal experiences and the many working hazards described to him by his father, the skipper of a boat. These stories and experiences made an indelible impression on his young mind and provided a rich store house for a number of his books. If you asked Caithness folk to name any of Neil Gunn's novels, I suspect that many would include "The Silver Darlings," arguably one of his best works.

A film company (I have forgotten its name) decided to make a film of "The Silver Darlings." I well remember the film unit with all its paraphernalia arriving at Lybster. As a number of extras was required for the scenes being shot along the Reisgill Burn and Lybster harbour, the company enquired at the school to see if volunteers were forthcoming. There was no shortage of them at a shilling per day — good pocket money in the 1940s.

One of the film's scenes in which pupils took part stays vividly in my mind. The setting was on the shingle beach down by the lovely little harbour. Dozens of people scurried around shouting. Dogs barked. Actors became impatient. Pupils looking and feeling awkward stood silent. Suddenly it was "Take one." The actors, made up as tinkers, cavorted around a flickering fire in a drunken melee while the pupils, as film extras, performed a hand-clapping game.

Some months later there was great excitment as we boarded the bus to go to "the toon" for the world premiere of "The Silver Darlings." Surely the film would revolve around us? Had we not spent a whole day shooting at the harbour? Who would be the stars from our class? We shall never know. Some biased film-maker had edited us out!

Dabbling in History

EARLY ASTRONOMERS

IT is midsummer's morning and grey skies herald our longest day. As yet not a peep of sun to mark the solstice and the long haul on to winter.

Surely, midsummer day ought to be commemorated far more widely in the north. Apart from a barbecue at Braal, some midnight bowling in the towns and an even later session on the golf course in Thurso midsummer day, one of the most eventful in our calendar, will pass unnoticed.

This was not always so. Some 4,000 years ago in Caithness people were expressing a great interest in the movements of the sun, moon and some of the major stars and constructed themselves observatories whereby the positions of these heavenly bodies might be predicted. One of the best known and most accessible of these sites was laid out at Mid-Clyth and is now known as the "Hill o'Many Stanes". Why, "stane", I know not, as the word is not current usage in that area.

A site for observing the summer solstice is located at Cnoc Na Maranaich, some four miles north-west of Dunbeath, where looking from the standing stone on the hilltop you can view the sun slide behind a notch on the horizon as it bids its northernmost farewell and begins its journey south.

Last night (June 1976) two of us sat shivering by this great standing stone gazing at the far horizon and fancifully thinking that it may have been 3,000 or more years since folk in Caithness last came to this site to pay primitive tribute to the life-giving sun.

The shochads protested vigorously at our presence and maintained an exhausting hour-long display of aerobatics. A darting snipe drummed its disapproval to the lengthy note of the curlew. The sheep, unaware that it was only 15 minutes until sunset, turned their backs on us and loitered down hill to settle for the night by the deserted and ruinous township with the well-preserved corn kilns.

Time to get the cameras out and perch on a ledge of the stone to give proof to mankind that our early ancestors had the way and skill to track the movements of sun and moon. Shutters were poised to click as a black mass of cloud curtained the horizon and blotted out the orange sun. Cameras were packed away in silence — but surely the sun will come north again.

CASTLES

THERE are two considerable interruptions to the cliffed coastline of Caithness: Dunnet Bay and Sinclair's Bay. The latter forms a sweeping embayment with a dune-backed beach that extends for over three miles. The area of the bay, which has undergone considerable marine erosion lies in a syncline or basin. Inland from the sands glacial debris slopes smoothly from the low peat clad plateau.

Such is the wide-vistad backcloth to the succession of castles and stately mansions that spring tall from the green sward: Sinclair/ Girnigoe, Ackergill Tower and Keiss, both old and "new".

The writer John Horne described Girnigoe and Sinclair as the castles "par excellence.... and the noblest spectacle of the kind in the north of Scotland. The lonesome situation; the splendid ruin; the strong, upholding rocks; the wide bay - these conspire to form a composition found nowhere else so completely in Caithness."

The stark spectacular ruins of Girnigoe, dating to the latter half of the 15th century, still manage to convey an impression of strength as they stretch skyward from a peninsula sheared by geos. Even the peninsula was truncated by artificial ditching to add to the site's natural defensive qualities. Adjacent to, and landward of, the original castle a considerable addition was added in 1606 and given the name of Castle Sinclair. Towards the end of the 17th century the castle complex was fatally damaged by military attack.

Not far from Sinclair/Girnigoe and offering a total contrast in immediate environs is Ackergill Tower, a pleasing structure rising lightly from a gentle landscape. Its twin doocots add to the charm of the setting. The principal tower or keep with its 10 foot thick walls appears largely unaltered although the top floor and battlements are later additions.

Towards the northern end of Sinclair's Bay lies the old castle of Keiss, whose slim elegance seems to grow from the low cliffs of bedded sandstones. Keiss forms a Z plan with a central structure allied to two diagonally opposite towers. The property was ultimately acquired by the Sinclairs of Dunbeath, one of whom, Sir William Sinclair, founded the Baptist church in Caithness.

Landward of the old castle rises the "new" dwelling, whose oldest parts date to the middle of the 18th century. The 19th century additions by Bryce carry the characteristic stone carved rope above the main doorway.

17th CENTURY

AS early as the 14th century Caithness had been noted for the production of its grain. By this time Thurso had become a significant port, trading in grain with countries such as Denmark, Sweden, Norway and the Baltic. The importance of this trade can be judged from the fact that King David II passed a law that "ane common and equal weicht, quhilk is called the weicht of Caithness (pondus Cathaniae) in buying and selling, sall be keeped and used by all men within the realm of Scotland."

William Lithgow, who travelled to Caithness in the early 17th century, remarked on this county of plenty and of its people, "the most bountiful Christmas keepers that ever I saw in the Christian world whose continual incorporate feasting one with another beginning at St. Andrew's day ... till Shrovetide ... methought the whole winter-time seemed to me but the jubilee of one day."

In the middle of the 17th century troops of Cromwell were garrisoned in Caithness to maintain a wary military eye on the restless natives of the north. Another reason for them being stationed in The Chosen Land was that Caithness was the only county north of Inverness where a large number of troops could be fed from surplus produce.

Documents of the Mey Papers (1) dated 1659, indicate that Caithness must have been able to supply a considerable surplus of bere and oats and Calder (2) says that in 1668 no less than 1749 bolls of malt were brewed into ale in Caithness — "a goodly quantity considering the limited amount of population at the period in question." Making ale was so popular that even in the good-living parish of Reay a Brewing and Distilling Company was established in 1697.

In 1680 and 1688, and frequently in the 18th century, particularly severe famines afflicted Scotland and many families perished from lack of sustenance, but there is no evidence in the Statistical Accounts, Mey Papers, or for that matter in Parish Records to suggest that Want was rife in Caithness.

It has been suggested that in the North there was a particularly high return on bere and oats, e.g., the average yield for Scotland was twofold, whereas in Caithness a fivefold return of oats and a sevenfold return of bere were quite normal occurrences. The Old Statistical Account for Wick speaks of "as abundant crops as the ground could carry."

In harvest time these vast acres of ripe golden grain replete with natural goodness must have warmed the cockles of a homebrewer's heart. Such a thought revives the hope that a Job Creation Project might restore Thurso Brewery to production and nourish Caithness chiels with a beverage too good for any king.

1. "Caithness in the 18th century — J. Donaldson, 1938.
2. "A History of Caithness" — J. Calder, 1889.

DUNBEATH STRATH

LAST Saturday we stepped back in time, winding our way up the attractive strath of Dunbeath, seeing abundant evidence of valley settlement from prehistoric times to the 19th century.

Until the early 19th century the method of agriculture here as elsewhere in northern Scotland had progressed very slowly from the late middle ages with the land still divided on an "infield" and "outfield" basis, the straggling ill-kept rigs of the "in-by" running deep scars in the arable land.

It is easy to criticise the unscientific nature of the farming, but the tenants had such little incentive and so many arduous hours of work to perform for the middle man (tacksman) and the laird. Tenants were expected to perform "tilling, dunging, sowing and harrowing .... providing peat .... thatching .... weeding the land, etc." according to Sir John Sinclair (1795).

Some old maps provide useful documentary evidence of Caithness place names: one of the most valuable is Roy's map of the mid 18th century which shows clusters of small settlements along (among other places) Dunbeath Strath. Quite clearly there was a substantial rural population throughout the country at the time and Dunbeath valley was no exception. It is largely an empty strath now, the people long gone through a combination of their own choice and clearance. Roy's map shows that the strath still had land laid out in the ancient rigs in settlements such as Achorn and Nouag.

Then as now the landscape was largely bare with scrub woodlands in sheltered locations. Some trees such as birch would have been cut to provide cruck timbers to support roofs and regeneration of the woodlands would have been limited due to grazing animals.

The people of these townships could hardly have imagined that substantial tracts of Caithness (not Dunbeath Strath) would become planted with conifers as economists remind us that Britain imports nine-tenths of its timber needs. Conservationists have argued that the increasing population of private forestry coniferous planting is not the result of rational economic decision making, but simply a tax dodge, with the new plantations creating dull, if not ugly, factory forests. And so, the conservationist argument might run, vast tracts of land, important for a variety of wild life, are irreversibly damaged. And all for some wealthy individuals seeking to reduce their tax liability! Apparently the Royal Society for the Protection of Birds wants the tax system changed and more consultation held over any proposed planting of trees.

It does strike me as odd that you can have problems erecting a garden shed when it appears legally easier to plant thousands of acres of trees. Surely in an environment such as Caithness, with sensible discussion, co-operation and planning, there is enough space for hill farming and re-seeding, forestry, wild-life — and garden sheds.

THE GUNNS

T HE Clan Gunn Society recently opened its Clan centre in the old kirk of Latheron, sited in an exceptionally well cared for churchyard. The Kirk, well over 200 years old, has been pleasantly restored and tastefully laid out. Clan Gunn took its name from Gunni, a grandson of the swashbuckling figure Sweyn Asleifson, whose deeds are recorded in the Orkneyinga Saga.

The Clan, then, can claim descent not only from the Norse Earls of Orkney but also from the Celtic mormaers or chieftains.

The principal Gunn lands were acquired through Ragnhild, Gunni's wife, who inherited large estates in Caithness and Sutherland on the death of her brother. Ragnhild's grandfather was the distinguished Earl Ronald who had built St. Magnus Cathedral in honour of his uncle, the saintly Magnus.

An important core of the clan territory was formerly around the upper reaches of the Helmsdale River in "Gunn's Glen", or "Glean na Guineach" as it was known in their language, Gaelic. This strip of land was wedged between the country of the Earl of Caithness and that of the Earl of Sutherland. Up west lay the Mackay country, and ultimately the Keiths gained a foothold on the borders of Gunn country.

During the 14th and 15th centuries the Gunns were gradually

dispossessed of their once extensive lands and hemmed into the upper waters of the Helmsdale and parts of the parishes of Halkirk, Latheron and Reay. One of the most famous Gunns was George, a chief in the latter part of the 15th century. He was an officer of justice, a crowner. His insignia was a large silver brooch which he wore constantly, giving him the nickname of "Big Broochy". It is possible that Crowner George attempted reconciliation between the warring Gunns and Keiths. In 1478 (some claim 1464) it was agreed that 12 men on horseback from each clan should meet at St. Tear's, or Tayre's, chapel close by Ackergill. The 12 Gunns apparently arrived first and entered the chapel to pray. As they did so the 12 Keith horses arrived, with each horse carrying two men. The 24 Keiths are reputed to have rushed into the chapel and following a bloody encounter left all the Gunns dead including the Crowner and his four sons. After this massacre the Clan subdivided into three families, based in Kildonan, Braemore and Strathmore.

The Clan, however, did not forget the Keith treachery and in the year 1518 took their revenge when a grandson of the murdered Crowner led his men against George Keith of Ackergill, disposing of him and 12 of his men.

The Clearances, rather than the Keiths, were responsible for the final dispersal of the Gunns from their traditional lands to all corners of the globe. Since those days the Clan has been without a chief and, as far as I know, no claimant has come forward with the required proof of hereditary right .... Don't be surprised to read that the Keiths have been keeping all legitimate claimants hostage!

KEITHS & GUNNS

IN the vicinity of Dirlot near Westerdale the Thurso river cleaves its way in tortuous loops through the thick boulder clay and its overlying swathe of peat. Suddenly the river changes character, leaving its flood-plained floor for the constriction of a narrow gorge excavated in the ancient rocks, which here push their way through the flagstone floor. Running in towards the gorge are some dry valleys which terminate in small terraces perched above the river, indicating the former level at which the water flowed, perhaps thousands of years ago.

As a result of its vigorous erosive work in the gorge the river has left an isolated pinnacle of rock, which, at least since the middle ages, has been utilised as a defensive stronghold. On the summit of this stack was located the ancient castle of Dirlot which appeared to grow out of the living pedestal of rock. The supposed builder of this ancient stronghold was a nobleman Sir Reginald de Cheyne who is believed to have fought with Bruce at Bannockburn and was one of those present at the signing of the stirring Declaration of Arbroath. There is a story that a drawbridge connected the castle to the valley side, but this appears unlikely because of the wide gap. Near the base of the stack is an artificial stony mound which appears defensive. It seems more likely that access to the site was gained by a removable ladder. Following the Cheynes the castle was occupied by the Gunns, Sutherlands and Mackays.

There are a number of savage conflicts associated with the area, including one where a party of Keiths, following a bloody encounter with the Gunns at Strathmore, proceeded to Dirlot castle, then occupied by the Sutherlands. Three Gunns, however, decided to follow the Keiths and at nightfall one of them ascended to the ground level apartment where he could see the Keiths quaffing ale and boasting how they had done the Gunns! In the midst of this boasting the chief of the Keiths approached the window, where he was mortally wounded by an arrow from the Gunn intruder who exclaimed in Gaelic, "Ionach gar n' Guinach gu Kaigh" — "The Gunns' compliments to the Keith!"

On this, the Keiths bounded for the door where there was a skirmish before the Gunns escaped under cover of darkness.

Some weeks ago I revisited Dirlot and looked in to the small kirkyard beside the gorge; stones commemorated Gunns and Sutherlands but I don't recall any commemorating the Keiths.

THE SINCLAIRS

THE Sinclairs are believed to have come over the Channel with William the Conqueror in 1066. They edged their way northwards and were soon a powerful name in Caithness, acquiring the Earldom of Caithness as early as 1455. An examination of Henderson's "Caithness Family History" reveals that of the 67 or so families owning land and having influence in the county, 27 were Sinclairs. Donald Grant in his "Short History of Caithness" related that

'E Sutherlands they focht 'e Gunns,
'E Gunns they focht 'e Sinclairs,
'E Sinclairs focht 'e wild Mackays,
'E poliss focht 'e tinklers.

The Sinclairs would fight the Gunns, Mackays or anybody else who threatened them. They were also quite prepared to march on the offensive and did so as far back as the 14th century when Sir William Sinclair, a strong patriot and soldier fought so bravely at Bruce's triumph at Bannockburn that the King, in honour of his valour, presented him with a sword on which was inscribed "Le roi me donne, St. Clair me porte", i.e. "The King gifts me, St. Clair carries me". Sir William was later killed in an encounter with the Moors in Spain, while accompanying James, Earl of Douglas to the Holy Land with the heart of Bruce. A century later the Sinclairs were on Flodden's fateful field in 1513, when James IV of Scotland quarrelled with his brother-in-law Henry VIII and marched over the border into Northumberland with a large army.

William Sinclair, The Earl of Caithness, and 300 of his kinsmen fought on the right wing of King James and after many lesser men had fled, they fought valiantly to the bitter end. The Earl fell and scarcely a man (if any) survived the tragic encounter. When the Sinclairs left home on that fateful occasion they were wearing a green uniform and crossed the Ord on a Monday. Since then, according to tradition, no Sinclair ought to cross the Ord on a Monday, wearing green.

A further misfortune to the Sinclair clan took place in 1612 when Colonel George Sinclair crossed to Norway with a force of many hundreds. This force met unexpected resistance in the fiords and valleys and walked into an ambush which obliterated half of the Sinclairs. A translation of one of the Norwegian ballads composed in honour of the victory over the Sinclairs, opened with these lines:

"To Norway Sinclair steered his course
Across the salt sea wave,
But in Kringelen's mountain pass
He found an early grave"

SHIELINGS

P LACE name evidence reveals that summer bothies or shielings were at one time common on the hill lands of Scotland.

Each year, in May or June, people took their cattle up to the shielings to help preserve the grass close by the villages for the winter months, with the added bonus that excellent butter and cheese could be made from the rich milk of the upland pastures.

This transhumance, or movement of people and their animals to the summer grazings can be traced back in Scotland to beyond the 12th century. Place name experts derive this information from name endings such as — *shiel, ary* (gaelic airidh) and — *setr* (Old Norse). There is, for example, a place name "airigh" to the north of Lybster. Assery to the north-west of Halkirk may derive from Asgrim's erg, Asgrim's shieling. The place name endings of Dorrery, Halsary, Lieurary and Shurrery would appear to have the same origin.

In reflecting on the shieling system in the north of Scotland we have to remember that the agricultural emphasis was not on sheep, but black cattle, for which there was a great demand in the markets of central Scotland and England.

In most parts of Scotland the shieling system seems to have disappeared by 1800, but in Lewis it lingered on until after the First World War. It is believed that a strong factor in the breakdown of the system was the gradual encroachment of permanent settlements up the slopes of poorer land and many "airighs" eventually became crofts.

Before the migration of families up to the shieling, the men had to go out as an advance party to repair walls and roofs that may have deteriorated over the winter.

There was great excitement in the villages when the eagerly awaited day arrived, not least among the children, who were spared the drudgery of school. The older cattle, too, sensed what the commotion was all about and on release from the byre headed straight for the shieling. Following the animals came the men, women and children strung out in a long column all heavily laden with goods and chattels.

The interior of the shieling hut was soon tidied, fresh heather and grass brought in for bedding and the comforting glow of the peat fire and its heavy scent soon dispelled the musty air. They would all retire early on the first night.

There was plenty of work to do next day: milking cows, making butter and cheese and sometimes, too, milk had to be carried to the village where the men returned to re-thatch the croft and make the hay. And many of them went far and wide to hunt the silver darlings.

Life for the youngsters in the shieling was one of uninterrupted bliss and the long barefooted days of summer seemed unending. But no longer do their happy feet patter around the stone huts on the desolate moors. No wild joyous laughter echoes in the hills or rolls along the lochans. Only the shochad and snipe dwell there now; the children have gone.

DIALECT

I was recently reading (legitimately!) a letter from a lady in the USA to a friend in Caithness. The former castigated the abysmal level of their Independent Television and said how much people looked forward to BBC programmes, which, she thought had less of a "standardising influence on customs and language". I don't think that I would agree, believing as I do that all the mass media have greatly assisted in standardisation and that this is particularly evident in the decline of dialect usage, which so coloured and enriched the use of everyday language.

Recently I was telling an incomer how one can visualise size in a sequence such as: boy, boyag, boyagie, wee boyagie, peedie wee boyagie and added that in so many dialect words the very sound seems to imply its meaning. Words in this category, I suggested, might include:

Aantle: to persist in whittering or arguing, e.g. a child persistently pleading with its mother to buy sweets.

Breenge: to lunge.

Claik: to gossip. The use of this word seems less offensive nowadays.

Cloor: a skelp. A "cloor on the loog" was a standard form of discipline before Dr. Spock and psychologists were invented.

Cyard: a person to be despised.

Drummoid: feeling downcast.

Flachter: agitated fluttering, e.g. the result of a fox getting in to a henhouse.

Glounk: water gurgling in a bottle. It can also be applied to a person drinking from a bottle.

Gomeral: a foolish person.

Gushel: clumsy and untidy person.

Mogre: to make a mess of or stir vigorously sleeves rolled up to the elbows.

Plowter: walk heavily as in mud.

Rownk: knobbly, e.g. "rownks o' knees.

Skook: walk with a bent motion, perhaps with an implication of slyness.

Skutch: move with haste and industry, as in tidying the house in a hurry.

Slounk: a lazy and somewhat sleazy character.

Soch: draw breath with difficulty.

Stravaig: wander all over the place.

Swack: active and athletic.

Trachled: dead beat, "fair trachled" being a common expression.

Trosk: feckless unreliable character, often with a likeable streak.

Middle aged and older readers may still have these words as standard elements in their speech, but how many teenagers, I wonder, still roll these riches from their Caithness tongues.

KIRK & DRAM

F ROM some of the records of the Highlands in the 18th century you would glean the firmest impression that drinking, dancing and immorality were the chief recreations of the people.

For instance in December 1758, the Kirk Session of Wick, to its self-righteous horror, was informed that Donald Robertson, a local joiner and keen fiddler induced people to his house for dancing and merriment and an intent to drink. Such meetings were deemed to be of a disorderly nature and the offending fiddler was banned from giving any further recitals.

In 1787 Wick Town Council following a complaint from the Kirk Session decreed that any musician providing music at an assembly was liable to be fined £10!

Earlier in the century the Caithness Presbytery expressed its horror at the profanity and drunkenness at weddings which gave occasion "to promiscuous dancing." In their lofty wisdom they declared that £3 surety was to be obtained from both the bride and bridegroom's family as a pledge that the wedding would be conducted with all due decorum!

Such blandishments of the Kirk appear to have gone largely unheeded as the subsequent meeting of Thurso ministers records "the manifold heinous God provoking abominations of all sorts abounding among all ranks .... outrageous drunkenness in the vilest degrees, horrid cursing and swearing."

Canisbay Kirk Session in 1710 complained of "keepers of ale houses who entertain such as are absent from divine worship," a practice which is still mildly popular!

During part of the 18th century the Sabbath in Caithness became of little account to many people. Parish records relate a case of drinking during the sermon. Did the sermons drive them to drink?

Perhaps the mushrooming growth of stills in the county had something to do with the drunkenness which seemed to be on the increase. Certainly the Justices of the Peace who met in Thurso in 1776 thought so as they agreed to discountenance as far as in their power, the pernicious practice of distilling whisky, so very prejudicial

The Thurso River cutting a narrow ravine at Dirlot.

The tortuous road through the lovely hamlet of Berriedale.

A beautiful setting for the Dunbeath Games.

A peaceful summer evening on Loch Calder.

to the morals and constitutions of the people, there being from 80 to 90 stills in the county.

The gentry, who might have been expected to show a good example to their tenants were no better, but perhaps more discreet! One of the most generous of hosts was James Sutherland of Langwell who, after dinner would whisper in his servant's ear "John, slack a dozen corks of wine,then go downstairs and take your dinner, and when you have done, come up and slack another dozen."

THE CROFT

"A croft is a piece of land surrounded by rocks and regulations," a Hebridean wryly observed.

In the Highlands and Islands the croft seems part of time immemorial and not an artificial creation that typified the early 19th century.

It comes as a surprise to recall that despite the ills (real or imagined) inflicted on crofters over many generations it took until 1985 before they formed their own Union. 1986 is another significant year on the calendar as it marks the centenary of the published report on The Napier Commission whose conclusion was described as "more sympathetic . . . and more advanced in its recommendations than was generally expected." It signalled a retreat for the rampant commercial landlordism which had turned large acreages of the Highlands into deserts.

Clusters of deserted crofts are particularly obvious in the parish of Latheron where the visitor can observe the traditional and distinctive single-storeyed dwelling which had domestic and non-domestic accommodation in a linear form.

It has been argued by Geoffrey Stell* that three major stages in the building history of this type can be identified. The first of these he identified at Torbeg, about a mile north of Dunbeath.

A second stage in the development seems to be marked by an increased size and complexity. In place of a timber screen, a stone-built partition might be erected between the byre and kitchen. The replacement of the open hearth to a mural fireplace can normally be ascribed to this phase, as can separate entrances for people and domestic animals. During this second stage the linear building could exceed 100 feet, as at Laidhay, now a croft museum.

Sometimes additional units were constructed at right angles to the

*Caithness: A Cultural Crossroads. Ed. J. R. Baldwin 1982.

original giving an interesting layout as at The Corr to the north of
Latheron village.

A further stage in the development of the croft layout is
distinguished by the complete physical separation of the dwelling
and the steading.

Some of the old barns and kilns still survive to illustrate the
distinctive building styles that evolved with the aid of local rocks
which split so readily into workable slabs of stone.

The drying chamber of the kiln took the old beehive form, the outer
walls gradually converging on the summit. About six feet from the
kiln base beams were laid across and on these smaller pieces of wood
and straw were laid in sequence to make a bed for the oats. . . . It was
all too easy for the unwary crofter to set his straw on fire and burn the
entire building to the ground.

FLAGSTONES

The remarkably regular geometrical jointing, the
beautifully layered nature of the bedding and the durability of
the flagstones have for many centuries proved of great service to the
people of Caithness. In fact, the use of flagstones is of such antiquity
that our Stone Age ancestors used the fissile slabs in the construction
of their burial tombs some five or more thousand years ago.

Although the excellence of the stone as a building material had for
so long been known, it was not until the early quarter of the 19th
century that it was commercially exploited on a large scale due to
that tireless (and under-praised) agricultural reformer, Sheriff Traill
of Castlehill. By 1825 paving stone was being shipped from the
harbour and within a short time the work force rose to 300 with trim
little cottages being built at Castletown to house the workers. Some
other proprietors had followed Traill's example and flags were
exported from Thurso and Scrabster as well as from Castlehill.

Apparently the best quality flags were obtained from the limey
beds which varied from a few inches to several feet in thickness. The
method of working these beds was to drive into the rock outcrop as
open workings, progress being as far as the removal of the "tirring"
(the overlying unwanted rock) would permit. No blasting was
employed, but each layer of overburden was carefully removed until a
large working area of pavement was exposed (Holborn Head quarry
being an excellent example).

The naturally occurring joints in this pavement were then forced
open by wedges and the flags carefully prised off in layers by means of

levers used with great skill and patience by experienced workmen. The shaping and finishing of the flagstones was originally done by hand before the large plants of cutting and polishing equipment were established at Thurso. Such a mechanised process can still be seen at Spittal quarry.

Over a century ago the Caithness Flagstone and Quarrying Company produced a publicity booklet giving details of their operations in the county, the extent of their trade and a list of published letters testifying to the quality of their quarry products.

At that time they had 15 quarries with eight sawing and polishing works. Already the company had shipped products to 42 towns in England, 41 in Scotland as well as to Ireland, many Colonies of the Empire and South America. Most of the major rail companies used Caithness flag on their station platforms and some of Britain's famous docks were paved with the grey slabs.

Nowadays the streets of the county are increasingly lined with concrete as the limitless durable slabs of our homeland are discarded and replaced by a short-lived synthetic agglomerate that is an insult to Caithness feet.

DUNNET BAY

A small westerly was whipping along Dunnet Bay on Sunday urging the charging waves to greater effort. Their pounding on the gently shelving sand has revealed some rafts of peat formed before the existence of the chain of dunes that adorns the neck of the bay.

Dunnet Bay, the terminus of a major depression in the Caithness plain, has a number of streams flowing into it, subdividing the dunes into separate units of quite variable size. The considerable quantity of fresh water reaching the beach possibly explains why its lower sector is so wet.

It seems likely that the links of Dunnet were common grazings until they were allotted to adjacent farms in the early 19th century. By 1840 the minister of Dunnet could write that the stability of the dunes had increased with this new policy of land division and protection. In the 20th century the Forestry Commission obtained tenure of large areas of the dunelands and a policy of consolidation of planting has left a distinctive mark on the Dunnet area.

The Old Statistical Account (O.S.A.) of the 1790s mentions the loose sand around Dunnet Bay which drives inland "frequently hurting the neighbouring land." Adjoining the bay is "a tract of barren land, nearly two miles in diameter, which is said to have been arable ground, or rich pasture . . . about the end of the last century. The ruins of cottages are now appearing in different parts of it; but they seem to be of a much older date." Along the shores to the north of Dunnet Bay, as well as in the parish of Canisbay, kelp making was important in the late 18th century.

The O.S.A. claims that Dunnet Bay "affords excellent flounders and haddocks and is sometimes frequented by shoals of herrings . . . in the harvest are amazing shoals of sellags (young saithe) which are taken in a small sweep net."

When the New Statistical Account (N.S.A.) was written in 1840 Dunnet Bay still abounded "with haddocks and other white fish . . . and there are occasional shoals of herring in the bay."

The population of Dunnet parish grew rapidly in the early 19th century. In 1801 it was 1366; in 1831 it was nearly 2000 people. The biggest increase was in the 1820s when "about 300 Highlanders from Assynt and Strathnaver, who had been removed from their possessions by the introduction of sheep farming, came to the parish." The writer of the N.S.A. ruefully comments that while the malting and brewing of ale is still carried out, "the severity of the excise law prevents people from a liberal use of this wholesome beverage."

R.L.S.

R ecently I visited a household where a young lad was avidly watching the film "Treasure Island." He diverted his gaze briefly from the TV screen to inform me that the author of Treasure Island, Robert Louis Stevenson, had at one time stayed in Wick.

Indeed he did, but I doubt if Wickers have ever forgiven him for his caustic comment on the royal burgh: "the meanest of men's towns on the baldest of God's bays." The author may well have had a twin prejudice towards Wick, as he had come north in poor health and left in a worse condition. Moreover, the failure of his father's breakwater at Shaltigoe was a bitter blow and all the worse because of fishermen's predictions about its short life.

Suggestions have been made that Ben Gunn in "Treasure Island" was based on a Caithness character. There does seem a good chance that he selected the name if not the personality from Caithness.

One of the people with whom Stevenson became quite friendly was Maggie Newlands or "Peggy Soo," with whom he had many a yarn at the pilot house above the braehead. Years after the departure of R.L.S. Peggy Soo informed local people, "what a fine gentleman he wis; he gi'ed me sixpence for whisky!" It seems to have done her no harm as she survived to a ripe old age. I have also heard it claimed in Wick that it was Peggy Soo and her clay pipe who introduced the disgusting habit of smoking to the fair sex of the county!

Another source informs me that Peggy Soo was wearing the plunging neckline long before the fashion houses of Paris had discovered it! Having said that she could never claim to have been a leader of fashion in Wick despite the attempts of salesmen to persuade her to spend money on clothing rather than on whisky.

One of these "specialists in ladies' attire," as he chose to call himself, was a well-known Wick character of the later 19th century called John Forbes. According to an article written by James Sutherland*, a former Pulteney postmaster, John Forbes had a powerful intellect and could discourse on any subject before a literary or debating society. For nigh on 50 years he was a regular attender of Wick's Mercantile Debating Society and often had the distinction of leading a debate.

One frosty evening, having taken a dram too many, he slipped and crashed to the ground. On somebody going to his assistance he was heard to exclaim, "Oh Lord! I have broken Thy commandment and John Keith's teapots."

PULTENEYTOWN DISTILLERY

Although distilling spirits from grain is one of the ancient arts of man, its origins are lost in the mists of time. It has been written that the first people to distil were the Arabs, an idea that depresses me as I have long held the romantic notion that the Picts developed the art and that the Celtic Druids held all the secrets of the whisky-making craft.

Whatever the origin of the "barley bree" Scotch whisky has now become the most popular spirit in the world and worth hundreds of millions a year in exports alone. Overseas demand continues to rise but home consumption is beginning to fall in the face of competition from other spirits and the Government's punitive taxation.

The Gaelic for whisky is "Uisge Beatha" and it is a corruption of the former word that is used today. The earliest reference to the making of whisky in Scotland is found towards the end of the 15th century, but it is likely that crofters lovingly distilled bold John Barleycorn long before that date. The era of the illicit still was officially brought

*In Caithness Your Home — Herbert Sinclair 1930.

to an end in the 19th century when licensed distilleries became established, with a concentration of them in areas where water came "off granite and through peat."

One of the oldest distilleries and the northernmost on the Scottish mainland is Pulteneytown Distillery, established over 150 years ago by Mr James Henderson who for 30 years previously had been proprietor of a small distillery situated farther inland. The water supply came from Loch Hempriggs and barley initially from Moray and Ross-shire and latterly Aberdeenshire. The distillery achieved a considerable production and a century ago produced over 80,000 gallons a year. During the Depression the distillery was closed but reopened in 1951 after a 25 year shut down. Most of its product goes for blending, but some is bottled as "Old Pulteney," thought by connoisseurs to be a whisky of high quality.

Queen Victoria is reputed to have given a fashionable boost to the popularity of Scotch. She may even have sampled Old Pulteney, a dram fit for any queen.

THE OLA

IT is very likely that the earliest peoples to come to the Chosen Land of Caithness did so by sea, having gazed longingly at the superb panoramic views of the northern Highlands from the warm lowlands of Moray. The highway of the sea took many groups of settlers to Caithness, including the Vikings, whose heritage is so marked in the place names of the most productive land on our county.

No regular communication by land with the south could be established until the road network was improved. With the introduction of a good road link to the south in 1819 a mail service was established between Huna and St. Margaret's Hope, a short crossing that may have been a link between Caithness and Orkney from ancient times and revived by vessels such as the Souter's Lass.

The first regular mail service between Scrabster and Stromness was established in 1856 and continuity has been maintained since then with, in more recent times, excellent service being given by a succession of St. Olas.

Last Thursday evening I crossed from Stromness to Scrabster in the most recent model, introduced last year, and equipped with stabilisers to counteract a rolling motion. For nearly an hour we sailed in the sheltered water of Scapa Flow, protected from the rigours of the weather by the great bulk of Hoy.

Passengers, many of them German and French, strolled on the

deck. The noise of chatter and laughter was everywhere; the monstrous one-armed bandit clanged continuously, with people gathered round it impatiently waiting to lose their money. What a queue there was for the hot pies!

The Ola turned Cantick Head, met its first sea, shuddered involuntarily, and plunged into the next one as if intent on a wild revenge. The level of conversation quietened. Soon there was no one to feed the bandit's hungry throat. The pie queue vanished. Where space permitted travellers with anxious faces stretched out on the seats.

The boat charged on, heading towards Mey before turning westwards to Dunnet Head with its great sandstone slabs fretted by chasms and geos. The seas were sullen and heavy by the lighthouse, contemptuous of the frail sea craft of men.

Five minutes from Scrabster pier conversations buzzed again and pale faces registered life. The loudspeaker crackled in an anonymous voice: "P.&O. hope that you have enjoyed your crossing."

MONTROSE

IN 1650 the Marquis of Montrose sailed from Orkney to Caithness, landing at the Bay of Sannick near Duncansby Head, hopeful that he could persuade a substantial number of people to follow him in the King's name. He persuaded all the ministers to take an oath of allegiance to His Majesty apart from the Rev. William Smith, minister of Bower, who was bound with a rope which was then fixed to the stern of a boat and dragged through the sea for a mile. He underwent this ordeal repeatedly but still refused to take the oath.

Ultimately he was taken, half dead, into a room where Montrose gave him an ultimatum: kneel to the King or be put to death. The minister replied that he had a message from the Lord to Montrose that "within nine months you shall be taken and dragged as dishonourably as I, and a thousand shall gaze on you for every hundred that has looked at me; and you shall die in the evil cause you have in hand!"

The chastened Montrose left William Smith in captivity and headed south. He successfully besieged Dunbeath castle and briefly stayed there. (His accommodation has a plaque "The Montrose Room" above the door.) He then marched along the old coast road towards the Kyle of Sutherland where he met a crushing defeat near the site of Carbisdale castle. Montrose became a fugitive fleeing westwards where he was eventually held in custody by McLeod in his

16th century castle of Ardvreck in Assynt. Following a show trial Montrose was beheaded in Edinburgh.

The Commission of the General Assembly on hearing of the defection of Caithness ministers arranged to have them cited to the Assembly.

The year after Montrose's abortive coup Cromwell's troops arrived in Caithness. The troops placed a strong garrison in Ackergill Tower. In the old kirk records of Canisbay mention is made of the "Inglishe horsemen being in our fields". Tradition has it that the old bridge adjacent to John O' Groats Mill was built by Cromwell's men.

The stay of the foreign troops was brief and things quickly returned to normal, the clergy concerning themselves with a woman who was swearing, a boy from Freswick who climbed a rock on a Sunday, another lad who collected eggs on the Sabbath and folk who lit a fire on the same day.

The elders and clergy, however, met their match in John Walter of Duncansby who swore for the minister, the bishop and the local schoolmaster, to whose salary he had been asked to contribute.

CLEARANCES

"THE Clans are gathering, gathering, gathering ...." From distant corners of the globe, fellows with the Christian name of Wilbur proclaim their Scottish ancestry, devotion to the ancient homeland and adherence to a clan whose kinship is exemplified by a particular tartan or tartans.

Glasses will be clinked at the many happenings romanticising and glorifying a past that to many of the participants from overseas seems to have been an idyllic age. Those who bother to take the time scan majestic mountains and the broad sweeps of hills that lord over the snug verdure of empty straths and glens. What beauty! What peace! And no people to spoil it. The people have gone. Gone over the endless black of the ocean to a world beyond their ken.

"I say Wilbur, look at all the greenery on the valley floors. Thousands of acres of it. What a waste! I suppose these Highlanders are too idle to use it. And fancy them not wanting to stay in a beautiful place like this. They must be a strange people, although I would hate to say so up here."

Wilbur is silent, eye sweeping along a furrowed crag where two burns weep their tears of history into an endless pool of time. Its waters are dark and deep with mysterious eddies, some gentle, some violent. Violence is a discordant word here where the hand of God has been so bounteous with natural beauty.

Ba! Ba! Na caoraich mora, the big sheep, has invaded the valley. Run! Before the big sheep. Gather your goods, Run! No time to take away the rafters of the cot. Run! The factor is coming. Stay! Stay! There is the minister with him; all is well. Or is it. Go? Go? he says. The will of God? Surely, it cannot be. The solemn ministerial face nods gravely and turns to the comfort of a substantial manse. It stands high on a hillock above the empty cottages.

Wilbur! Wilbur! What on earth are you staring at? You find these derelict cottages moving? I don't! They give me the creeps. I feel as if I am not wanted here, as if a thousand eyes are staring at me. Come, Wilbur! Come! The Clans are gathering".

The Halkirk Parliament

EARLY DAYS

THE Halkirk Parliament* reassembled this weekend following a short summer recess (a much shorter one than at Westminster) What a democratic Parliament the village has! No Prime Minister, no Cabinet, no Party Whip, no agenda and never a vote on anything. Anybody in the Community can become a Member and attend meetings. But meetings do pose a problem as you cannot predict when one will take place. Meetings just happen — at the football pitch, by the bridge, near the paper shop or, occasionally during this thirst-quenching weather, in the hostelry.

Debates arise from issues of national significance or items of local news, or sometimes both — e.g. the current water shortage. Following the lengthy and customary serious discussion we were able to offer the drought-stricken southerners some advice:

Drink more whisky;

Emigrate;

Give up washing (some hitch hikers we pass appeared to have done so);

Import bottled water from Caithness (we have plans to tap the pipeline from Loch Calder. Surely it would make little difference to the lochy?).

This water shortage has plunged some members of the village Parliament into deep gloom, as it has prevented that monarch of fish, the salmon, from holding court in all reaches of the Thurso River. What a shame, we concluded, that "toffs" should be paying out so much money and not even see a salmon, far less catch one. Our

---

*Born in the mid 1970s.

greatest sympathy, however, lay with the poacher who has had as
lean a year as most can remember.

Many of us this Easter had decided to keep plenty of room in the
deep freeze as one of our pundits predicted an abundance of salmon
coming from the Caithness water courses. The odds on his being right
are dwindling with the Thurso river so low that, apart from the dark
pools, you can walk across it where you please. No, despite the
forecast of a salmon mountain, I cannot see us having the same
complaint as a group of Aberdeenshire labourers, who, two centuries
ago, raised a court action against their landowner for giving them too
many salmon by way of payment for their services.

NO WOMEN!

O H-dah! Oh-dah!
Another day's antics begins at Westminster. A wifie drones on.
There are a few Members in the Chamber; most are comatose. Of the
635 M.P.s the majority are in the tea or beer bar waiting for the
buzzer to summon them to vote on an issue in which they have no
interest, no knowledge, no participation but had to obey the party
line. It all adds up to democracy (with a small "d").

You could argue that Westminster is more democratic than the
Halkirk Parliament, which has no women members and does not
intend to have any! I have been advised to stress this point, as, with
the election of Mrs T. a gaggle of Halkirk females have threatened to
gate-crash our next meeting and chain themselves to the beer pumps
of the Members' bar. The ghost of Lady Pankhurst is alive and well!

I was requested last week to reveal the Membership of the Halkirk
Parliament whose activities, declared the enquirer, were more
secretive than the Masons. Alas! the identity of the Members' names
must remain a closely guarded secret, but, as a sop to modern trends
of open Government a recent meeting declared that it will permit a
press photograph to be published by the "Groat" and "Courier". This
exclusive world scoop will be made available to the local press on
condition that no names are published and that details are not
revealed to the "New York Times", "Der Spiegel", "The Observer", or
"Press and Journal".

I write these lines on June 7, a dreich day and climatically well
suited for European elections which, despite our apathy, seem to me
to be more important than the British ones. The era of the "Little
Englander" has gone; all recognise this except the British whose

politicians still harp on about "making Britain great again," "taking our rightful place," "giving a lead to the world!".

It will be interesting to see what strides the European Parliament make towards democratising the bureaucracy of the Market's Commission. During their first Session many great issues will come up for consideration and the way political winds in the village are blowing, high on the agenda might be "Rights of Women to the Halkirk Parliament". But I have great faith that the doughty chiels who constitute the membership will resist such an imposition and that we are unlikely to hear our next meeting open with a strident female voice uttering ....

Oh-dah! Oh-dah!

BIRDS AND GAMES .

I T is 3.38 am. How on earth can a being come to life and erupt into tuneful song. A blackbird did this morning and likely does every day, but even a sleepless chiel like myself cannot guarantee to hear this daily opening fanfare of the dawn chorus.

What does one do about sleeplessness? I have tried traditional remedies like a dram (or two) each night, a hop pillow, counting sheep, going for a walk, not going for a walk, not taking a dram, and neglecting sheep. "Why not try work," suggested an aspic Member of Halkirk Parliament.

The village had noted a certain edginess about the Parliamentarians lately as the July centenary Highland games approach. Wives are finding unwashed dishes by the sink, carpets unhoovered and benign mothers-in-law threatened with the garage as a living area.

Film stars and politicians who have successfully scaled the greasy pole will be aware of the stresses that lie heavily upon the worthy Members who have to seek sponsorship, attract entrants, make a thousand arrangements and above all organise the weather so that the public can enjoy the world's best pipe bands. It's not easy, especially the weather part, so anybody reading this column who has recipes for keeping away the rain clouds should get in touch with the Games' Meteorologist who has been known to misinterpret the tea leaves in the cup on more than one occasion.

As D. Day approaches I suspect more of the Parliamentarians will be hearing the dawn chorus and getting so little sleep that you could recognise them a day or two after the games as the bedraggled fellows with red-rimmed eyes and zombie-like countenances, ready to stab at you on the slightest provocation.

Speaking about stabbing: a pair of terns who are nesting nearby take the utmost umbrage if I get too near their domain, voicing their displeasure and diving towards my head with sharp beaks. Birds look after their offspring better than folk! Like the mother partridge we watched last week flachtering around in a ditch trying to distract our attention while her two chicks scuttled across the road to the safety of the long grass.

The bird song everywhere is rich and resonant just now, particularly the soaring notes of the lark and nowhere better than on Lybster golf course where the aerial choir is incomparable. An hour of soothing music may be just the tonic I need to combat lack of sleep. On the other hand if that worked I would miss the blackbird's reveille. Nature like the Halkirk Parliament, is not easy to keep up with.

WEATHER MEN

I T transpired that many members of the Halkirk Parliament had recently taken the notion to study the weather charts produced each evening on BBC television. The upshot of this has been that their conversation is now peppered with meteorological jargon such as "a depression is moving in from the west," or, "an anticyclone is located over central Europe."

The more serious minded can adorn such generalisations with technical details: "I note that yesterday's warm front has become occluded," or, "that temperature inversion should give us a dull sky this evening."

Some of the more cynical of our membership place little reliance on the BBC's weather computer data from Bracknell and place far greater faith in Radio Orkney's morning contribution. However, an even greater reliance is given to the indications of nature: for instance, the rooks are building their nests higher in the branches this year and that is a sure indication of a good summer to come. The fact that the nests are at a higher altitude because of the mild weather or an increased number of rooks has been contemptuously dismissed.

Some swallows appeared close by the village at the beginning of last week and have been cavorting at great speed in search of insects. Their agitated activity has been interpreted as further evidence of the good summer.

The most curious argument for balmy days in June, July and August came from a Member who has spent some days (and nights) observing a rat at close range. He has attributed its boldness to this

stationary high pressure system and further prognosticates that
Halkirk wifies will spend the summer strolling around in their
bikinis. No sooner had this Member completed his meteorological
observations of the rat's behaviour than he shot it, rather thrilled
with his accuracy at four yards' range!

As a canny chiel I am rather reluctant to accept these
Parliamentary findings, but on Friday I had a curious experience
that made me wonder. While passing Rumster on the way to Lybster I
noticed something on a fencing post, stopped the car and stared into
the unblinking eyes of a wild cat. He sat looking at me for ages before
agilely bounding from his perch and melting in to the forest.

"There ye are now; ye've seen the evidence yerself! Wild cats don't
behave like that normally. Surely that's concrete proof of a good
summer to come."

I hope that the Honourable Members are correct for I have already
made an advance booking for three weeks' holiday in July on the
Costa del Braal.

COWLD

I should have anticipated the recent and sudden onset of Arctic
conditions, having been forewarned by Nature and a few decrepit
members of the Halkirk Parliament.

Even more reliable portents of early wintry weather were
Parliamentarians who had throbbing chilblains in October. Did not
the milkman sleep in for the first time, hinting at an early
hibernation for the village?

It is really unkind of the weather gods tc inflict the first sharp bite
of winter so early in the season.

The drumming wind stuck stubbornly in the north bringing its
stinging icy arrows to our unwary lowland. By morning a quilt of
snow had settled over stubbled fields. Along the seashore the anger of
the sea splintered on the steel coast. Even our shadows seemed hard
in the cold sun.

The radiance of winter is best appreciated through a window from
the comfort of a centrally heated room, its temperature augmented by
the rich warmth of a log fire. That is the way to experience this robust
weather. Siberian wastes are for Siberians and not for Caithness
chiels whose body and soul have long lost the battle for adaptation to
winter's iron grip.

I often wonder how we survived childhood on minimal heating (and
lighting) and shivering bones laid on a distorted caff seck or lumpy

horse hair mattress. Gaps in the window frames were plugged with old rags. The breath came like smoke from your mouth. You lay cocooned in layers of inherited blankets while the faint flicker of the small oil lamp lazily fell on the cold green distemper of the walls.

Here's to progress. I raise my warming dram to the inventor of electricity.

UNDER THE MISTLETOE

R ecently I took a brisk stroll along the south head at Wick; nobody else was mad enough to do it on such a raw day, with long grey rollers charging towards the breakwater. Returning by the harbour I passed a huddled group of retired men.

"Ah wish ah wis lek a hedgehog, I'd hibernate."

"But ye'd miss Xmas and New Year, Jock!" I did not hear Jock's reply.

Xmas does draw ominously near with local Parliamentarians feverishly searching around for original gifts for their Managements (wives). Many of us share a Member's view: "It's not easy to be original when ye're over 45!"

Some of the Members in a seasonal burst of optimism have already ordered their mistletoe, which was originally hung to drive away spirits. I have never been aware of any of the worthy Parliamentarians wishing to send away spirits! Far from it. To many of them spirits have a certain magnetism and are an essential ingredient of the season of goodwill.

Nor will you find them eloquently extolling the beauties of the mistletoe's glistening ice-white berries and exquisite foliage ... rather, will you discern the misty memories in their eyes ...

The mistletoe seems to grow best on apple and its appearance on oak trees may well have tempted the ancient Druids into leafy glades; its religious and pagan associations would appear, therefore, to go far back in time. Many ministers, over the years, have banned the hanging of mistletoe in their churches because of the Calvary legend or the association with paganism.

In some households it is considered unlucky to hang mistletoe indoors; others will not have it in the house before the 25th of December. Members of the Halkirk Parliament do not subscribe to either view. By the end of the week their back and front doors will be decorated with the magical berries and every time the bell rings you can be sure they'll charge to answer it in the hope of a bonnie lassie on their threshold.

ACCENTS

"I like coming north to Caithness but find it embarrassing to converse with the locals. I can't understand them! They speak so funny and fast." And this coming from a Yorkshireman with an accent as thick as his county's pudding!

I'll accept his criticism for some parts of Caithness where speech is rapid and spoken in a monotone: to a stranger it must be like facing a verbal machine gun. In the south-east of the County, say, from Ulbster to Berriedale the speech is slower and more deliberate and most folk use "the" instead of "e". Not true Caithness, you may argue, but at least comprehensible to a sooth-moother!

Last summer, a Dounreay employee was declaring that if you heard a chiel talking loudly and noisily in a local hotel, he must be from Wick. If from outside the county he'll be from Glasgow, he added with a grin.

We had a visitor last month who spoke harshly of the Buchan brogue. Having lived among it for many years I confess a warm attachment to it despite the manner in which the folk seem to massacre language.

What accent, our visitor enquired, did I like least in Scotland, and I found, to my surprise, that I could not answer him. What I intensely dislike, and many appear to agree with me, is the substitute posh voice that many Scots deem necessary to please or impress people. Some of the worst offenders are announcers on BBC TV and ITV enunciating their speech in tones alien to them; it is a public declaration that somehow their own tongue is inferior and unfit for public consumption. They provide the worst examples that come to mind of the inadequate Scot.

I then added that I felt most sympathy for folk with a "pheasant" accent whose speech always strikes me as a studied mimicry of somebody else. There are a host of adjectives that spring to mind to describe the vocal outpourings: metallic, abrasive or grating and all too often (but perhaps quite unintentionally) offered to the listener in the manner of master to servant. Some households deliberately cultivate this "superior" speech; certain public schools avidly promote it and colleges of two well-known English universities have been known to look askance at the provincial accent.

Did this mode of speech arise to distinguish the ruled from the rulers and is it, to some degree at least, perpetuated to impress the natives? Mercifully, it impresses few in Caithness.

Now we really ought to do something for folk brought up and tutored in "Pheasant" speech and so I propose that a Finishing School be established in the county for the elimination of la-di-dah accents, marbles in the mouth, touches of the pan loaf or other vocal afflictions. It will be run by Members of the Halkirk Parliament who are renowned for their impeccable elocution.

Tangling with Nature

ROOKS' PARLIAMENT

January's snows still cling tenaciously to the ground. It is time Mother Nature waved her weather wand and released us from the icy talons!

Despite the intense cold our robin still alertly patrols his territory scolding noisily at intruders, especially the blue tits who are sharing his menu at every opportunity. The aggressive robin met his match yesterday when some black-headed gulls appeared, sent him packing, and devoured "his" lump of fat. He voiced his disapproval to the world but no feathered friend came to his assistance. Such is the way of the wild — and mankind.

Early yesterday morning a nearby rook struck up a solo. Within a minute there was a deafening raucous racket from his companions. Whether they were joining in chorus or expressing their displeasure is hard to say. The general result was like something from Top of the Pops, except that the songsters of the trees did not have the absurd appearance of their human counterparts.

The rooks frequently hold their Parliament in the field behind the house where they assemble with an air of formality, sometimes in a crude circle with an offender placed in the middle of the throng. Amid such cawing, stabbing of the ground and flachtering of wings justice is dispensed and the court adjourned. Then, many of the participants wing to the nearest fencing post to sit in brooding posture.

Although I have not witnessed such a happening, I heard a naturalist declare that if an assertive rook took it into his head to build a nest in advance of the colony's collective approval, his fellow rooks would assemble at the offending home and argue fiercely, giving the offender a wigging with the warning that the planning committee might not be so lenient next time! Sometimes a bird builds its nest at a considerable distance from the rookery. Is this a punishment to a persistent offender who has crossed the awesome authority of the Regional Council once too often?

The rook has a curious social and domestic behaviour. For days he will happily consort with his mate but then take the notion to abandon her to enjoy the camaraderie of his cronies. Just like the Members of the Halkirk Parliament at weekends!

BIRDS' WEATHER

Thursday 16th February, 1984. Despite the gentle but prolonged thaw there is still ice on Loch Rangag. A pair of ducks home in on the pond, gaze forlornly at its frozen surface and wing westwards. A solitary buzzard patrols about Latheronwheel Strath. He has hunting opposition today as a peregrine cuts the horizon and arrows its way down valley uttering its sharp "kek, kek, kek".

What a handsome fellow he is with slate-grey plumage, heavy black "moustaches" and barrel chest with a buff tinge. What power his slight frame generates, hurtling through space towards an unsuspecting victim. How glad this elegant hunter must be to see winter's coat disappear.

Has spring come? "I widna say", as a crony responded cautiously. There are a few signs of Mother Nature beginning to stir. Green spears are thrusting through the dull brown soil including the colourful harbinger of spring, the crocus.

Botanical buffs have informed me that the crocus is not a native plant but an import from Holland during the latter half of the 16th century when there was considerable commercial bustle between Britain and Europe. We'll all look forward to the radiant crocus gladdening both mind and eye in the bleak landscape.

What beautifully crisp evenings and awesome skies we have had during the past week. Excellent owl weather! Their hoots echo among the leafless trees and roll away to the hills. Ghostly galleons they are, cruising through the ocean of the night. The effect is quite eerie and sometimes distinctly startling. I am thinking particularly of the short-eared owl that perches on the post near the garage and waits till I am a few yards away before launching himself from statuesque anonimity into the shadowy night.

His nightly predations may not be as successful as of yore as a pair of field mice have taken refuge in the garage from the cold weather. Maybe I do him an injustice. He may know of their change of accommodation and waits patiently by the fencing post for the furry patter of tiny feet.

MAY

The shy, maidenly snowdrop has yielded prominence to a chorus of daffodils trumpeting their golden approval of May. The hawthorn, having less faith in the whims of our weather, opens a few cautious buds to the heavens, where clouds still prowl with dark mischief in mind. Along the hedgerow a cold wind sings among the lifeless beeches.

But there was nothing lifeless about the late evening last week when a million Merry Dancers skipped along with abandon against the dark purple backcloth. What extraordinary formations they displayed; sometimes strung out in swaying streamers, occasionally forming arches and frequently arraying themselves with strictest military precision. And all the time the colours varied from pale yellows through greens to fiery reds converging in feathered brilliance high above the land of Caithness.

The Merry Dancers, Northern Lights or Aurora Borealis — call them what you will — are most frequent in the higher latitudes surrounding the North Pole in a wide, oval belt. The brilliant luminosity of the Dancers is the product of electrical discharges in the atmosphere and there is a marked correlation between the colours produced and the charge of the current; for example, salmon-coloured tints are always close to the positive source. There is a close identity between sun spots, magnetic storms and Auroras, the appearance of a large spot on the sun being accommpanied by magnetic storms.

I wonder how our primitive ancestors interpreted these awesome heavenly displays of interchanging lights? Would they have cowered in their huts or huddled terrified in the recesses of caves? Perhaps to appease these fearful gods they threw offerings in to lochs or assembled by some sacred stones where powerful priests uttered incantations to Nature's dancing searchlights.

Maybe the sombre stones of Achavanich encompassed folk fearful that the end of the world was nigh. I wonder if, in those distant times, depressed-looking chiels wandered around the countryside proclaiming that the world would end in ten days time?

Whatever our predecessors felt about the Aurora Borealis, they would have taken little heed of the "electrical discharges" theory. What an unpoetic explanation! As a loon I believed that Merry Dancers were formed when the pale, romantic light of the moon was reflected from gleaming ice caps on the starry vault of the heavens.

BIRDS

A cutting north wind is bending our sycamore like a slender bow. Is this really the beginning of June? Are we only three weeks from the longest day?

A quartette of swallows balanced on a nearby power line must be wondering if they have mis-read the calendar. An aggressive arctic tern seems more belligerent than ever, appearing to dive at anything that moves. The house martins are too busy to have noticed the weather while the fertile chattering starlings are noisily feeding their offspring and fouling everywhere.

A blackbird has built a nest in the garden and spent ages sitting on it, but not an egg has appeared. I have not seen her for a couple of days: maybe she has gone into hiding until the general election is over!

Early yesterday morning (around 5 a.m.) I watched a curious ritual taking place in a field behind the house. A handful of rooks were strutting around and stabbing the ground from time to time as they moved in circular motion by a small pool of water. They took turns of stepping into the shallow water and splashing it around themselves before leaping out to vigorously shake the feathers dry. Those who had washed flew away while others replaced them to join the small group at their social ablutions.

A contrast to the ragged rook is the smartly attired wood pigeon, the Beau Brummel of Braal who sips water and takes his bath with a studied solemnity.

The hawthorn hedges, flushed with green, house the colourful male chaffinch and the dapper greenfinch, often mistaken for a yellowhammer. In ancient days the hawthorn was held in considerable repute, particularly in the Mediterranean where people used it at their marriage festivals, with flowers as a bridal crown and the sharp branches to form processional arches. In Ireland it is still regarded as unlucky to cut down a hawthorn, as the "little folk" are there to protect it.

The hawthorn is only one component of our hedging, making attractive contrasts in colour, particularly with the copper beech. The specimen in our garden is thrusting its bronzed way skyward but, like our solitary sycamore and the forlorn swallows, must be wondering when summer will come.

SUMMER

"**H**urry up, boy, or you might miss the summer!" shouted a crony, as I hauled out of the garage a variety of implements that could loosely be termed golf clubs and headed for a not-too-vigorous nine holes on the Costa del Lybster. A few days later the normally quiet course was hotching with ambitious players eager to win the open first prize of a week-end in Paris. We had already been to the French capital and so did not bother to enter . . . . although an offer of 24 handicap (for each nine holes I trust) did briefly stir the mercenary instincts.

Having failed once more to conquer the course I hastened home for further conquests of the armies of weeds that march ceaselessly across the arable plot. How were the cabbage, cauliflower and sprouts doing? Not too well. The pigeons, which I recently rashly referred to as the Beau Brummels of our wood had attacked and almost devoured all three species. Resignedly, I turned to a large rectangle of ground in which I had sown grass seed the previous evening to find that a squadron of sparrows had taken tenancy of it for dining and recreation facilities. They stabbed furiously at the seed and scuffed the dry earth around their feathers.

"Try tying lengths of string with strips of plastic attached", said a helpful acquaintence. I did and it has not deterred our feathered friends, but has attracted an over-fed cat who scrabbles around the patch flicking his paw at the plastic strips . . . . All I need now is a mole.

The unseasonal weather has not inhibited the trees or hedgerows: our young sycamore is swaying lithely in the wind casting a constantly moving shadow. The two ash trees scarcely break up the light as the slim leaves are spaced so far apart that they all but fail to cast any shadow at all. Even more open is the willow, its supple strength yielding to every whim of the wind.

The wind! The wind! It is the constant music of Caithness. Even when weather forecasters deny its existence, Caithness folk know that it is lurking round the next corner. It will even follow you across the county as we discovered on our next golfing safari to Lybster. As we set off for the first tee sudden gusts materialised from nowhere and brought in their wake huge plumps of rain.

TRAIN JOURNEY

I am sitting huddled in a B.R. compartment. Frozen. Through the frosted glass I can see a poster with a smiling Jimmy Saville proclaiming that "this is the age of the train". It is cold comfort. Still the railway seems my only hope of returning this week to The Chosen Land as aircraft are grounded and many of the roads in Aberdeenshire are blocked.

The buffet at Inverness station offers some warmth, hot pies and chilling pop music which a glowing Caithness chiel and some cronies are enthusiastically trying to drown with a raucous rendering of "Flower of Scotland".

The train leaves Inverness, barely an hour late. It threatens to come to a standstill at Beauly but heaves into life just as expiry seems inevitable.

What a wild and primitive beauty is about the landscape. Great heaving hills of white, cut by green battalions of conifers. How delicately chiselled are the birches, bare-boughed and frost rimed, angular lines carved against the smooth dunes of driven snow. A quiet untarnished white world slips by the metallic charge of the train.

Here and there we pass an isolated deer, stark in the snowy waste. A startled herd of thirty deer have to interrupt their anxious search for a meagre breakfast under the thick blanket of snow. They seem less forlorn than the sheep, heavily larded in snow and gazing intently to distant cold horizons.

Near Altnabreac there is a flurry of grouse, tiny and vulnerable in the white wilderness. What a sight for German sportsmen who now strike fear into the hearts of Highland ghillies. This year, it seems, the Germans shot more ghillies than grouse! Next year the lairds will be releasing the statistics of how many brace of local peasants the shooters have bagged!

The bustle of activity on the platform indicates that we have arrived at the busiest rail junction north of Dingwall. This is Georgemas! A naval lieutenant sticks his head out of the carriage window. "Good heavens!" he exclaims "How on earth can any sane person live up here."

"Excuse me!" I said, "This is where I get off!"

WEATHER AND NATURE

Friday: Last night's equinoctial gale left some damage in its wake at the Costa del Braal. It must have been even more frightening on the Cairngorms, with gusts of over 150 mph, which according to a national newspaper was a Scottish record.

I suppose the weather gods were entitled to conjure up something nasty for us following the flawless skies and remarkably peaceful weather of February, when it seemed so unreal watching successions of charts proclaiming foul forecasts for southern England while the far north basked in an Indian summer. Bad weather now and again is good for folk who live in the stockbroker belt!

I felt particularly sorry for the rooks this morning as the waning gale removed the last vestiges of their patient nest building from the skeletal hands of the deciduous trees.

More successful has been the diligent effort of an industrious thrush whose half-built nest in a trembling spruce survived the buffeting wind. For some days we have been trying to feed the energetic nest-builder but are continually thwarted by the alert, chattering sparrows who are expert at diving in to, and hiving off with, any morsels on offer.

We are fond of the darting colour flashes of the greenfinches who restlessly stab around the garden for any suitable sustenance. Some of the local mousehounds (cats) are aware of this and stealthily stalk the finches, occasionally making an unwelcome kill.

The snowdrops survived the storm intact, their shy demeanour foxing the most turbulent twists of the west wind. They make a cheering contrast with the forceful blue of the crocuses. Green spires are everywhere as the daffodils shrug off the lifeless cobwebs of winter for the sharp promise of the spring air.

AUTUMN

Caithness had had an unusually prolonged autumn, with occasional leaves still clinging to branches. Some years, if low temperatures and strong winds coincide, I have seen the trees stripped bare by the end of September. This year the "season of mists and mellow fruitfulness" had been extended giving us as varied a colour to the foliage as we are likely to see.

The chills of November have their compensation as the pearly dawns give rise to the vast violet vault of heaven where the evening stars hang with stunning brillance. Silver light from the silent moon falls on the geometry of the fields, its cold luminosity frosting the furrows of the new ploughed land.

Our rook colony seems noisier than ever, floating over the fields in immense flocks to perch in military precision along the fencing posts by the wood. The rooks can sit statuesque, often for remarkably long periods and then suddenly, as if by some telepathic signal, they rise in unison.

They greatly outnumber the wood pigeons, whose softer tones are often lost in their neighbour's unmelodic chorus. The wood pigeon seems a more purposeful character, flying quickly from field to woodland as dusk approaches, the air a-rustle with the flachter of its wings.

Often small groups of starlings alight among the rooks or pigeons, darting everywhere and chattering with an irritating persistence. The bigger birds seem quite tolerant of them; not so the two robins who have taken over our garden. They give the starlings no peace and constantly harass our resident blackbird whose mornings of quiet undisturbed breakfasts have been rudely shattered.

The hare in the field behind the house has acquired his winter coat; what a handsome fellow he is in his thick tawny jacket. When you see him scuttle across the ground it is hard to believe that he can crouch almost unseen among the brown tussocks of grass. Countrymen have told me that hares will use the same form for years; they are also excellent swimmers and will readily cross streams or rivers to get at tasty morsels on the far side. I fancy that it would be a chilly swim in the Thurso river this morning as a cold south-easter whips across the valley.

Local Tales

WHISKY FROM HEATHER

When would the first home brew in Caithness have been made? Did the Stone Age farmers who built the impressive burial tombs know the secret? Perhaps it was these ingenious stone and metal workers called the Picts who first concocted the heady potions. Certainly the Vikings knew the art and the sagas inform us that they went to considerable trouble to obtain good quality malt for brewing.

Some hold the view that there is a genuine tradition of Pictish ale in Orkney, basing their argument on the fact that the wild oat which infested the islands into this century was known as "Pict's aits." This primitive cereal was believed to produce a fine quality ale which never caused drunkenness. In Holinshed's Scottish Chronicle (1578) he observed that the Orcadians were the "greatest drinkers of anie man in the world; yet was there never drunken or man disguised with drink seene".

There is also a tradition in the making of heather ale/whisky in Orkney, Shetland and Caithness. In Orkney, legend says that the last of the race to know the secrets of the recipe were captured by the Vikings. The father agreed to give the secrets to his captors provided his son was not there to witness his treachery. The Vikings led the boy away and killed him, whereupon the father proudly declared that torture might have wrung the secret from his son, but his lips would be permanently sealed.

Yet, a recipe of sorts for the brewing of heather ale survived into modern times. A highly intelligent old lady informed the late Ernest Marwick* that as a very young child she would be sent out on a summer's morning to obtain green heather tops for brewing. She knew that there was some special reason for gathering the heather at this early hour, but could not remember what it was.

---

* The Folklore of Orkney and Shetland — E. W. Marwick, Batsford, 1975.

From Latheron parish comes another tale of a man who made potions from heather.** He lived in a farm close by the old broch on the shores of Loch Rangag. The farm house had a secret whisky bothy built in to its gable wall, with an adjacent stream flowing under the barn. Another of the secret stills was set in a broch, perhaps the one by Loch Rangag.

Tradition gives its final occupier as Grey Steel, the last man who knew how to make whisky from heather. Alas! He and his sons were foully murdered by a band of men from Watten to whom he refused to tell the secret.

To this day the old broch retains the name of Greysteil's castle. I wonder if the ancient still survives inside? Perhaps with a sample of the delightful heather whisky and a copy of the recipe! What a boon to the county it would be, considering our bounteous gifts of heather and peat. Maybe by 1992 the deserted russet moorlands of Caithness will be studded with stills producing the rarest of amber dews and an inner warmth that will long outlast the liquid gold from the grey North Sea.

THE COAST

The landscape glories of Caithness lie along its 105 miles of coastline with a variety to suit all tastes. If you are looking for great sweeps of cliffed grandeur then head for the iron coast of Bruan about halfway between Wick and Lybster. Here the great wafered sandstone rocks have been hammered by the unremitting sea to produce spectacular geos, gloomy caves and pinnacled stacks. The lonely coast attracts large numbers of sea birds who can readily establish multi-storey colonies on the tiered sandstone sediments.

The wild corrugated shoreline offered protection to man as well as seabird, with the fragmentary ruins of two castles, both associated with the Clan Gunn; Castles Halberry and Gunn, the former perhaps being the most recent.

A steep buttress in this area was dubbed by Gaelic speakers the "Leac na oir" — the rock of gold, following a tale of treachery and cruelty relating to the site . . .

A Caithness chieftain, said to have possessed lands and a residence on this coast (Castle Gunn) wooed and won a Scandinavian princess who consented to make Caithness her home. As the time of the

---

** A History of Latheron District — S.W.R.I., Caithness Books, 1968.

marriage approached, it was decided that the ceremony should take place in the bridegroom's residence. And so the bride embarked for the land of her adoption in a vessel laden with a dowry of gold and precious jewels.

Alas! The Caithness chieftain appeared to be more interested in the dowry than in the lady and using the pretence of securing her safety, he arranged that a bright light should be shone on a stretch of shore to which the vessel might be steered with confidence. But the treacherous, greedy lover fixed the light on a dangerous precipitous cliff. In the dead of night, with no stars about the sky, the bride's vessel struck the fatal rock and in a few tragic moments disappeared beneath the relentless waves. All aboard perished as no hand was offered to help.

The chieftain roared his delight and next day sought his wealth from the ill-fated ship. In vain. The treasure remains, awaiting collection by some astounded Caithness fisherman who has accidentally shot his nets inside the three mile limit!

STROMA

According to tradition*, on a beautiful summer evening about the middle of the 15th century, a small boat left a large vessel off the eastern point of Stroma and made its way for the shore.

Apart from the crew rowing the boat there was a man and woman who, from their appearance "seemed to be persons of some quality or distinction". The man was in his mid thirties, the woman some ten years younger.

The boat was almost full with the strangers' luggage, consisting of trunks and boxes, among which was a large chest secured with double hoops of iron and so heavy that it took six strong men to carry it ashore.

As might be supposed the arrival of two such individuals in the island created a considerable stir. The strangers were very reserved and had little communication with the islanders. Obviously they were not short of money and paid liberally for everything they required.

The strangers spent much of their time strolling around the island, usually in the afternoon, and seemed quite captivated by the sunsets.

Months passed and the cloud of mystery still lay over the strangers

* "Sketches from John O'Groats in Prose and Verse" by James T. Calder, Wick, 1842.

until suddenly news rushed round the community that they had purchased the whole property of the island. They then lost little time in building themselves a substantial residence and their own chapel, where they worshipped devoutly. The man, particularly, attended to his devotions which he often concluded in a flood of tears.

The locals wondered what might be the cause of this melancholy which the comfort of religion seemed incapable of removing. Some folk concluded that he must be guilty of a terrible crime and began to look upon him with distrust and distaste.

Matters continued in this vein for some years until one evening, tongue loosened by too much indulgence in the juice of the grape, he gave the following account of his background: "My name is Kennedy. I am a native of Scotland who was obliged to leave my home area because of an unhappy love affair. . . . I had a rival whom I challenged to duel and killed him by the sword. Panic-stricken I set off to sea in an open boat hoping to escape to England. However, a storm blew up and the following night I was picked up by an English pirate ship near the Bell Rock. Some months after joining the crew I learned that the young woman who was the cause of my unhappy duel had died of a broken heart.

After many piratical adventures the captain died and I was elevated to the command. We now cruised for some years in the Mediterranean and acquired a great deal of wealth. One of the ships we attacked had a beautiful lady on board who agreed to marry me if I would abandon my piratical life. I chose this small island on account of its remote and solitary situation; and here I mean to pass the remainder of my days in making up my peace with that just and good Being whom I have so grievously offended by my crimes."

BY DUNNET BAY

The great sweep of Dunnet Bay is defended by the extensive sandstone wall of the headland which is trenched by a number of narrow ravines or geos and little creeks, one of them being Gitterygoe.

During the summer of 17-- a young lad searching for some stray cattle observed a small boat coming into the haven, having set off from a large three-masted sailing ship. As soon as the craft touched the shore a young lady of some twenty years alighted and then shouted to the disappearing crewmen "My William that they say was drowned will be back . . . . and we will be married".

Astonished at what he had seen and heard the boy, forgetting his mission to search for cattle, dashed home and related his story. Several of the neighbours hurriedly followed the boy to the creek where they gazed silently on the stranger pacing along the beach.

Throughout the summer and autumn she remained among the rocks, living on seaweed and any scraps of food brought to her. With the onset of winter she was obliged to find shelter at nearby cottages, where despite enquiry her story remained a mystery. Her sole revelation was that she come from Greenock.

After many years had passed a beggar in sailor's garb called at one of the cottages on the west side of Dunnet seeking quarters for the evening. He soon fell into conversation with the landlord, a fisherman, who enquired if he had been this far north before.

"Only once, and connected with an affair of a distressing nature. Have you seen or heard of a female who was put ashore among the rocks twenty-five years ago?"

"Yes", replied the fisherman. "I was the person who first saw her when a boy of fourteen. She is still alive, goes under the name of the Greenock Wife but now wanders up and down the country in a state of mental derangement."

"I thank God that she is still alive", replied the beggar. "She was put ashore by her father, the captain of the vessel, who bitterly resented her association with the Mate and determined to banish her. After this deed her father became more of a recluse and addicted to the bottle. One evening while we were sailing towards the Danish coast in heavy seas, the captain appeared on deck trembling. He then exclaimed "I am a murderer. Hell is yawning open to receive me." So saying, with one fatal spring he leaped into the boiling sea. The Mate then took command of the vessel which was later wrecked on the island of Bornholm. Of the crew of fourteen hands only myself and another escaped to tell the mournful tale."

Such was the beggar's story. The unfortunate Greenock Wife continued to wander through Caithness. She died at an advanced age and was buried in Canisbay Kirkyard.

THE FOOD RIOT

So many people in the Highlands and Islands were living on such tiny patches of land that by the early part of the 19th century they had become dependent on one crop for the family sustenance — the potato. In many communities the potato was the staple diet for nine months of the year. (The common tattie first appeared in the

Highlands in the middle of the 18th century and was certainly common in Caithness before 1800.).

In Caithness the summer of 1846 was a mixture of fierce drought and torrential rain. Through it all the shaws flourished and a bumper crop was widely predicted. But then, in early August the air-borne spores of fungus stole silently over the Moray Firth; overnight the shaws darkened and withered. The potato crop was dead. The crop met a similar fate the following year.

People were starving. Relief did come, slowly, from a Government more concerned about property than people. In some ports there was the terrible irony of undernourished and gaunt people watching boat-loads of grain make their way to the markets in the south. It was too much for some folk.

On 20th February the Sheriff of Caithness sent an urgent plea for soldiers saying that a mob was planning to scuttle a grain ship at Wick. The official response was prompt. Two companies of troops arrived by steamer, landed at Ackergill and headed for Wick in aggressive military display, drums beating and bayonets fixed.

Some soldiers were placed on the wharf to guard the ship; others marched briskly to the meal store where carts were being loaded with sustenance desperately needed by starving people.

En route to the harbour the carts were halted by a barricade of men who rained stones on the troops. At last the Sheriff read the Riot Act and the troops surged forward. A bitter and ugly struggle ensued during which men and women were wounded by the bayonets before they broke ranks leaving the meal carts and boat to the military.

When loaded, the boat set sail, the troops formed ranks and marched towards their quarters. Again the mob set about them. Captain Evans Gordon ordered his men to have muskets at the ready and he then shouted a warning to the crowd. They replied with another hail of stones. The troops fired, aiming high, but some of the falling shot caused injuries in the crowd.

The following week Captain Gordon and his men were marching towards Thurso to quell another food-riot. In London well-fed politicians shook their heads. Would Highland peasants never learn to respect property?

PENTLAND FIRTH

The Pentland Firth has the unenviable reputation of being one of the most turbulent stretches of water around the lengthy coastline of the British Isles. The Admiralty North Sea Pilot contains some pieces of advice to mariners, including "even in the finest weather the transition from smooth water to broken sea is so sudden." Sea-tossed souls from Stone Age times to the present day can no doubt vouch for the accuracy of that advice.

Many a sailor (and day tripper to the County Show) has tales to tell of foul journeys from Caithness to Orkney but surely few can be as remarkable as that encountered by James Mackay, a native of Mey, in December, 1806. On Christmas Day of that year a gale of unprecedented violence arose from the north-west and churned Dunnet Bay into hills and valleys of boiling foam.

Such was the ferocity of the storm that large-scale damage to property occurred throughout the county. Many of the primitive dwellings of the poor folk were unroofed and stackyards were bowled over like skittles.

At the time there were a number of fishing boats anchored off Scrabster. Most of the men had gone ashore for the standard liquid refreshment and with the sudden onset of the gale had failed to reach their vessels.

Three of the fishing smacks broke from their moorings and were driven along Dunnet Bay. A sloop called the "Fisher" was hurled on to the rocks below Thurso East and remarkably no hands were lost.

The most incredible escape was of James Mackay whose smack ran to Orkney in the teeth of the storm. On board with him was a young lad whom James shut in a cabin to prevent him being washed overboard. After trimming his vessel as best as he could in the perilous conditions he lashed himself to the helm and by an incredible feat of seamanship made the Orkney shore. The exertions of his nightmarish voyage undermined his health and he died at the young age of 27.

A CAITHNESS WEDDING

In days gone by Caithness weddings could be dangerous as well as hilarious occasions. A "Northern Ensign" of July 1884 recalls such an event in the late 18th century when a wedding party arrived at the kirk to find another couple ahead of them. The minister called both parties to be united at the same ceremony. As soon as he had given his benediction the brides bolted for the door as tradition held that the first out of the church carried all the luck for the future.

A scuffle followed between the two wedding groups and a number of the men had their kilts removed! In the general melee Janet Gunn (now Janet Sinclair) managed to slip past and so was first out of the kirk, much to the relief of her brother Alexander a well-known strong

The long grey cairn at Camster where the dead were interred by Stone Age peoples some 5000 years ago.

The mysterious stone rows of Mid Clyth. Did they form a prehistoric observatory?

Caithness is the broch county of Scotland. The remains of this Iron Age broch (circular stone-walled fort) protrude into

Old Braal castle, Halkirk, dates at least to the 14th century.

The spectacular ruins of Castles Sinclair and Girnigoe.

Now the Clan Gunn centre, but formerly the 18th century church of Latheron.

The lovely old dwelling of The Corr, near Latheron.

Lybster, surely one of the most picturesque harbours in Scotland.

Spawning the salmon on Thurso River.

A cheerful group, despite a blowy crossing on the St. Ola.

How many drammies, I wonder? Pulteneytown distillery, Wick.

The lovely setting of the Langwell Gardens.

man. Alexander mustered his party and called upon his piper to play the pibroch, "The Gathering of the Clan Gunn for Battle".

That night the Gunn and Sinclair families celebrated the wedding with a splendid barn dance. While the festivities were in full swing the barn door burst open and in marched three red coats and a sergeant looking for conscripts for the army. Alexander immediately ordered them out and following a refusal picked them up one by one and threw them head over heels outside. The sergeant shouted that his master, Captain Sutherland of Wester Loch, would soon right this affront. Soon after the challenge was issued the angry captain "put himself under a vow and oath that he would have the satisfaction with his broadsword when he would meet Alexander at Spittal Hill market".

Captain Sutherland had the reputation of being one of the best swordsmen in Scotland. Little hope was given for Alexander who armed himself with a big cudgel and held a small crooked stool as a shield. The combatants began their contest and in the third round the captain's sword was shattered with a blow from the cudgel. The captain agreed that he had had enough, mounted his horse and rode off to Wester.

PRECENTOR AND BEADLE

In days gone by the parish of Reay was renowned for the quality of its precentors, who led the congregation in singing. Halkirk parish was not so well endowed according to a tale related about their precentor Tait, who was a gardener at Braal Castle. Tait sang so loudly and with such a large open mouth that a young lad named Iverach threw a stone into it which broke a number of the precentor's teeth and terminated the singing! Iverach took to his heels as the congregation folded into laughter. The culprit was eventually overtaken by two of Tait's sons seeking revenge for the injury and ignominy inflicted on their father.

The quality of Tait's voice clearly could not bear comparision with that of Alexander Macdonald chosen as precentor by the distinguished Reay minister Finlay Cook. The minister was so proud of his precentor that when he officiated in neighbouring parishes he endeavoured to bring his silver-voiced singer with him. On one visit to Thurso, so displeased was Finlay Cook with the town's precentor that he dismissed him after the first psalm and replaced him with Alexander Macdonald saying to him (in Gaelic), "Come here Sandy, they spoilt my bonnie psalm"!

After twenty years of leading the congregation in divine song in Reay Alexander Macdonald went to reside at Stonegun in Olrig parish, where, as foreman in the flagstone quarries he was held in considerable esteem by employees and employers. For many years he acted as precentor in Olrig Free Kirk whose minister was Alexander Auld the author of "Ministers and Men in the Far North".

Although the precentor was indispensable to the singing, the beadle or "minister's man" had a prominent role in the solution of day to day problems. Typically, the beadle had a sense of humour . . . Following a particularly heavy snowstorm a minister found he could not get to the town to buy snuff. That evening the beadle presented the minister with a small packet, remarking "I hope this will please you till the thaw comes".

"Bless the Good One who gave you this," replied the minister. The beadle, looking rather embarrassed retorted: "Man, ye'll no have to pay back this favour; I just went and swept the pulpit!"

PREMONITIONS

One of Donald Grant's many memorable poems is "The Ghost of the Hill o' Forss", a tale that began with Cheordie coming home "fair stottan" from a sale in Thurso. Taking pity on the grey ghost Cheordie offered him a dram and soon had the wraithe on the sad path of demon drink!

Reports of ghosts and ghostly occurrences in Caithness appear to have been far more common in bygone days. For instance, in 1849, six people died of cholera in Houstry, Dunbeath. Prior to this happening a woman reported seeing a moving bright light (a harbinger of death) issuing from some cottages and disappearing by an old meal mill. Such travelling lights were also believed to indicate the route of a funeral procession and folk thought it strange that the meal mill was the end of the journey. Yet, at that very spot four of the cholera victims were buried.*

From Halkirk comes the story of a miller who died and within a few days had returned to his old house, always disappearing into the "but end". This behaviour continued until one of his sons, who worked south, returned home and followed the ghost into the far room. The ghost pointed to some corn measures which were stored below a bed

* "Folklore Gleanings and Character Sketches" — G. Sutherland, Wick, 1937.

and requested his son to burn them. They were false measures and the miller's spirit could not rest until they were destroyed.

A parallel tale is related of a lady who kept a country inn in Caithness. She repeatedly haunted the inn until a God-fearing man from the district, equipped with Bible, questioned her. She immediately pointed to the whisky measures in the cupboard and asked that they should be destroyed. They were subsequently thrown over a high cliff into the sea. Her measuring stoups and gills were evidently false measures!

A man was crossing the rugged countryside between Braemore and Houstry when he saw an apparition entering the gate of Tutnaguail cemetery. The figure marched purposefully to the far corner where a ghostly figure shook hands with him before sinking down into its grave. A few days later a native of Dunbeath, who had been abroad for many years, died suddenly.

The man who had witnessed the apparitions a few days previously, attended the funeral and was astounded to see that the deceased was buried in the corner grave from which the ghostly figure had arisen. This proved to be the grave in which the dead man's mother had been buried many years before.

People from the Past

THE medieval bishopric of Caithness, it has been argued, probably coincided with the old Earldom, an area including Caithness and Sutherland as far as the Oykel river.

Andrew is the first bishop "who appears in authentic history" and mention is made of him in 1181 being witness to a document exacting a penny annually from every inhabited house in Caithness. Andrew had unfortunate successors in John, who was blinded and had his tongue removed, and Adam, who was murdered at Halkirk.

Then followed Gilbert, archdeacon of Moray. He seems to have been a man of abundant energy who supervised the construction of many buildings, including that marvellous castle of enceinte, Kildrummy, in upper Donside and the elegant cathedral of Dornoch which he had built at his own expense. "Even the glass for its windows was made on the spot under his own eye." There would seem a good possibility that Gilbert lived to see his cathedral completed as the Breviary of Aberdeen records "that he rests in the church which he built with with his own hands". Gilbert was created a saint with his festival held on 1st April. Gilbert is said to have performed many miracles including the restoration of his account books, burned by some vandals. A curious tale relates to another wonder. A certain man had hired the salmon fishings in Caithness, but owing to the lack of fish could not pay his rent. He earnestly beseeched Gilbert to wash his holy hands in the water to attract the salmon. Not surprisingly the river swarmed with fish .... There are a few eager casters around Halkirk who would pay handsomely for the Gilbert touch!

Like most saints Gilbert's relics were long venerated and it is known that oaths were made at least into the 16th century by touching "the relics of the blessed Saint Gilbert".

It could be claimed that Gilbert was the founder of some form of law

60

and order in darkest Caithness and Sutherland. An early record of Caithness quoted in Craven's "Diocese of Caithness" claims that he (Gilbert) had a "large share in civilising his rude provinces, in interposing between the vengeance of King Alexander (for his slaughter of locals after the murder of Bishop Adam) and the ignorant multitude .... and he deserved to live in the affectionate memory of his people as 'Saint Gilbert'".

POCOCKE

D R. Richard Pococke, Lord Bishop of Ossory, who was born c. 1702 made a tour through Caithness and Sutherland in the year 1760.

He approached the Caithness boundary from North Sutherland and was impressed by the splendid house of the Innes family at Sandside and the remains of a "Pict's house" (perhaps the one by Achvarasdal House).

At Thurso he was offered 'toasted ears'.

"What is that?"

"Why, the ears of a calf toasted on bread — and baked in a pot".

Apparently the worthy cleric enjoyed it and commented particularly on the excellent quality of the wheat bread, which he ate with great gusto, prompting his host, James Murray of Pennyland to exclaim "Stop, my lord, else your lordship will raise a famine in ye country".

After a brief stay in Thurso, Pococke crossed to Orkney, where he spent a week, returning to Caithness by the post route, landing at Rattar. Thurso, he noted, "is pleasantly situated on a bay and a river of the same name, which rises out of several lochs to the south-east towards Dunbeath. It is but indifferently built, and is chiefly supported by the salmon fishery. They also export some corn ...."

From Rattar he journeyed eastwards past the old parish church of Canisbay towards Duncansby Head "and Johnny Grott's House, which is in ruins." His party then climbed a vantage point to look towards the islands of Swona and Stroma. The former had a dozen families and rented for c. £15 a year. Stroma, which exported limestone to the mainland of Caithness, "had some thirty families and rented for £100 a year."

Pococke noted that in Caithness and Orkney the people had an unusual way of preserving their grain. "They make a foundation of loose stones five feet in diamater, lay chaff on it, and add a heap of corn in the middle, then they sett up straw on end all round the stones, and put in more corn, and as it fills they bind it round with straw ropes, and so continue raising the straw until it is about eight feet high, and they finish it in the shape of a cone, covering the top well with straw, and bind it round with such ropes of straw as they lay over their thatched houses. They have also a neat way of dressing their thatched houses in the roof within — I mean people of some condition. For about four feet of the lower part they lay flags, then on to the top ropes of straw close together and drawn tight. On others they lay the sods and then the thatch. There are two ways of laying straw — either regular, as they thatch in England or laid loose, and kept down with straw ropes, in which last case it is renewed every year. They make near the sea a compost of sods, seaweed, and dung, move it once, and then shred it off very thin to lay on the lands."

BAYNE

FOR some years I had planned to re-read the manuscript of Aneas Bayne which he wrote in 1735 on "A Short Geographical Survey of the County of Caithness". I succeeded last week.

The early part of his essay makes brief comment on each of the parishes which are often spelt differently from today's standard usage e.g Lathron, Wattin, Bowar, Canesbay and Dunnett.

The parishes of Wick and Latheron have good fisheries and Wick River, along with the Forss and Thurso, "furnishes good salmon fishing".

Mey "is one of the pleasantest villages in the North of Scotland" and nearby Stroma contained "40 families who maintain themselves by corns and fishing, which are indeed the two great commodities of this parish."

The lowland parishes are well served with corn, with Watten producing more hay than any other parish and its loch producing "great numbers of trout and sometimes salmon".

Occasional references to ministers' stipends suggest that they had around £50 a year with many "catechisable persons" to look after including 1300 in Reay, 1000 in Dunnet and 1100 in Halkirk parish, whose locality of Braal "is the most beautiful place in the whole shire .... and is adorned with three gardens". Even by this relatively early date in agricultural improvements in Scotland Thurso East was fenced by walls and hedges.

The section on trade stresses the volume of corn grain in the county: 16,000 bolls in any year are sent to neighbouring counties and shipped (mainly to Leith and Glasgow) and on to Norway. In addition to corn a great variety of goods (tallow, beef, port, ham, geese, hides, leather, calfskins, etc.) were exported from Scrabster, Thurso and Staxigoe.

There appeared to be a well established trade in black cattle to the south of Scotland and parts of England.

Bayne claims that prior to 1735 "there was a considerable fishery on the coast of Caithness, which is now in a great measure decayed for want of suitable encouragement". A fishery was "still encouraged at Clyth and Wick". The merchants of Caithness "furnish the country very well with iron, salt and other wares".

Bayne found "nothing barbarous among the vulgar or the gentry" and the clergy were described as "learned and well gratified men".

"The English language is generally understood .... and the Irish language (Gaelic) obtains most in the parishes of Lathron, Wattin, Halkirk, Reay and some parts of Thurso to the west."

"The progress of language will in a little time wear out this (Gaelic) language" which has "so long been a retainer to ignorance and barbarity".

Near Duncansby Head is a house called "John o' Grotts", descendants of "strangers who visited the shire". The family had "carved out their names on an old table preserved in the house .... unfortunately the names are razed".

A comforting conclusion was that Caithness "is allowed by all impartial visitors .... to be one of the best civilised shires in Scotland".

SIR JOHN

"HE is the most indefatigable man in Britain." Thus spoke a French contemporary of Sir John Sinclair of Ulbster, a man whose enormous vitality and ability contributed so much to Britain during the Age of Improvement.

Sir John was born at Thurso Castle in 1754 and inherited the family estates when only sixteen years of age because of the premature death of his father.

At the age of 26 he became a Member of Parliament and was soon in the forefront of debate on all aspects of farming. Due to his exertions the Board of Agriculture was established; only six years after entering the Commons he was knighted by King George III.

He was also an energetic writer. Among his publications was a "Code of Health and Longevity". Perhaps he practised what he preached as he was 81 years old when he died.

Of all his literary involvements the most celebrated was the First Statistical Account of Scotland, a comprehensive parish by parish account of the country for which historians and all interested in our past should be eternally grateful.

Sir John was a tireless promotor of new ideas. Occasionally his advocacy verged on the bizarre: for instance, he introduced Spanish sheep into Caithness and due to the damp environment he had them all equipped with boots! This fruitless experiment was carried out on the Langwell estate which he had purchased in 1788 for £9000.

To the same estate he then took a flock of 500 cheviots with border shepherds. As the flock expanded he became faced with problems of stocking and grazing with the 86 tenant farmers who lived in the lovely valley. According to Henderson* humanity required that about 500 individuals, who inhabited the estate, should not be driven from their ancient possessions, without having some other means of subsistence pointed out to them, hence it was necessary to proceed with caution, in extending the system of sheep farming, and to form some plan of provision for the people." The plan devised was to move the people from the relatively productive valley to the exposed infertile ground along the coast. Each farmer was to be given two acres of "potential arable" and Sir John was to employ each tenant for up to 300 days in the year, paying for the labour with grain and money, depending on the working days agreed on ....

.... Langwell Strath is long empty as is the bald inhospitable landscape where the evicted made their homes.

ROBERT DICK

HAVING taken his father's advice the young Robert Dick arrived in Thurso in 1830 to premises in Wilson's Lane. An oven was added to the site and Dick, the baker, was now in business. In between the long hours of making a living he immersed himself in the various wonders of his environment, becoming an expert in geology, palaeontology, botany, conchology and entomology. With due respect to fellows working at various establishments at Dounreay, he was the greatest scientist to have lived in Caithness.

His serious study of insects (entomology) began 150 years ago when he was 25 years old. Such was the dedication of the man and his intensity of application that within nine months he had covered large

---

*J. Henderson "General View of the Agriculture of the County of Caithness" London, 1812

tracts of the county and collected most of the insects found in Caithness.

In his work Dick used references with extreme care. His knowledge was acquired by working in the great natural laboratory around him rather than in assimilating extracts from the many authoritative works of his library, bought from the modest profits of his bakery.

Thurso folk must have been astounded at the behaviour of their baker who would appear from moorland, valley or beach, bedraggled and exhausted, to have a hurried wash and don his baker's apron before beginning his shift in the bakehouse. Genius has long since puzzled ordinary mortals! "How painfully, how slowly, man accumulates knowledge!" he wrote to friend and fellow-scientist, Hugh Miller of Cromarty.

Correspondence with Miller whetted his intellectual appetite. He entreated his merchant suppliers to send him books, packed in paper bags and buried in the sacks of flour.

When the weather was unfavourable he immersed himself in his beloved books. As soon as the sky brightened he was away to haunts old and new, sometimes as distant as Morven. Those who occasionally joined Dick on his sojourns found it an enthralling experience. Mostly he went on his own and appeared to enjoy the sweet solitude of his investigatory rambles. During the long days.of summer he often made journeys of 40 or 50 miles to see some favourite plant or observe an insect in its distinctive habitat. Even if caught out by a sudden change in weather Dick was reluctant to leave his studies and return to the town .... Along our iron coasts, soft valleys, bare hills and matted moors he worked with clinical application, never lonely in the society of Nature.

IAN MACKAY

ONE day in October, 1952, at school in Wick, a class-mate said: "Did you hear that Ian Mackay, the journalist, has died?" At that time I had never heard of the fellow; neither had the others in our group.

Ian Mackay, one of the three sons of a remarkable woman, was born in Wick in 1898. He was an avid bookworm and left school at 14, having already acquired a reputation for scholarship.

Some years ago a Wick lady told me that Ian, while part-time message boy, was so engrossed in reading one of Shakespeare's plays that he failed to notice he had crossed a road junction and crashed his bicycle into a wall on the other side of the street! For the remainder of his life he had an abiding passion for Shakespeare and was said to read some passages of his work each day.

During the 1914-18 war Mackay made his first contributions to journalism with sketches sent to the "Groat" and "Northern Ensign" from the trenches of France. After the war he continued his "Groat" articles with "Mac's Letter from a London Attic." Later, he obtained a post on the "Piano Maker," published by Herbert Sinclair, a fellow Wicker.

Mackay's journalistic base widened when he joined the London staff of the "Western Morning News." In 1934 he was appointed industrial correspondent of the "News Chronicle" and quickly won the trust of the Trade Union movement during one of the very difficult periods of its history. Already the associate of many leading political figures, the shaggy, unruly mop of hair of the brilliantly funny Mackay became a familiar sight at Labour Party conferences.

It was while covering events of the 1945 General Election that he evolved the format and style of contribution that made him one of the outstanding newspaper essayists of this century. In those essays he displayed the rare gift of communicating his bubbling personality to readers, each of his outstanding articles peppered with literary allusions that reflected the astonishing width and depth of his reading as well as an encyclopaedic memory.

It was a profound shock to his friends and associates when, apparently in the fullest vigour, he was suddenly struck down at Morecambe in 1952. Following his death letters poured in to the "News Chronicle" office from all over Britain. Readers who had never met Ian Mackay deemed his death a personal loss.

Idle Thoughts

FESTIVE CHEER

THE Press, Radio and TV, not to speak of the business world, give you little chance of forgetting how many inflationary days there are till Xmas. The whole nerve-wracking operation is artificially injected with the drama and tension of a Cape Kennedy launch. Perhaps it heightens your anticipation of the Festive Season!

The media and advertising agencies are having problems trying to make Xmas different. It is difficult for them when, for the majority of children, Xmas is any week in the year. And so to a novel suggestion: give the kids nothing on Xmas day — not even food. No, I don't suppose you find that acceptable. Neither would the business community.

In Thurso last week I overheard a small boy say that when he had decided on everything he wanted, he would write to Santa. A bike might be included in the list as the new one he was given last year was nearly a wreck.

In various shops adults, too, were having serious decisions to make: now, what kind of jewellery would she really like. That £10 pendant looks rather cheap. Do you really think he suits that colour of sheepskin jacket?

Earnest discussion could be heard as to whether these pains, the Bloggs, would send a card this year. Better buy a New Year card to have in reserve — just in case. Yes, that one with warmest wishes to two lovely people would suit. Should Aunt Clemency get a 'decent' present this year? I should think not. After all, the miserable baggage only gave the bairns a bag o' sweeties last year. See if you can find her something under a pound. Oh! come to think of it you know the blether she is. All the neighbours would hear how mean we have been to her and her with her ulcer on her bad leg. Yes, give her something "respectable".

Overheard near Woolies and freely adapted: "Willag, remember how annoyed we were last year: invited in to the Swindlebottoms (just to see their bigger Atomic house) and offered as many different drams as could be found on the shelf at the Portlands. Her and her "gin and its", A mere squiff of soda in whisky, darling" "and do give the Smiths a Tia Maria — we always have one after dinner". Look Willag, I know fine that they live oot o' tins and it's a can o' lager they have wi' their spam on a Sunday .... But I suppose we'll need to ask them over at New Year. Off ye go, Willag, and order a roast for New Year. Mind too and get some some o' that er, er. Och ye know the stuff I mean — we drink it efter dinner every Sunday!"

LOCOMOTION

E ACH generation of Caithness folk is assuredly getting softer; physically most of us have to put less effort into work and even socialising means setting off in a vehicle, instead of exercising our legs. The internal combustion engine has facilitated our communications and impaired our health!

Our bodily resistance to the climatic rigours of the North has no doubt suffered in this general decline. I doubt if we could withstand the conditions endured by our 16th century ancestors in Caithness who, according to a letter of the time, preserved in the British Museum .... "for boithe somer and wynter (except where the froest is moost vehemente) goynge alwaies bair leggide and bair footide, our delite and pleasure is not only in huntnge of redd deir, wolfes, foxes and graies, whereof we abound and have great plentie .... The delicatt gentillmen of Scotland call us Redshanks."

No! Shanks's pony does not get enough exercise. Few of us would be fit enough for employment as "currors" or foot runners, those loose-limbed lads of bygone days who carried letters or goods of value from one part of the country to another. The last of these "currors", David Allan, died in Halkirk in 1797.

This softness in our condition I have attributed to the invention of the motor car. Perhaps I should go farther back in history and blame it all on James, the 14th Earl of Caithness, who was a pioneer of mechanical locomotion.

As long ago as 1860 the good Earl startled the peace of the Highlands by driving north from Inverness in his new £200 steam-driven carriage which was built in the form of a phaeton on three wheels, capable of carrying three passengers sitting at the front and a stoker at the back.

The bottom of the carriage consisted of a huge water tank, capable

of holding 150 gallons. At the rear was storage space for coal. When
loaded the steam carriage weighed 2½ tons, a heavy vehicle on the
roads of those times, although the Earl claimed that it did them more
good than harm by ironing out the irregularities!

The journey from Inverness to Wick took two days, including the
many stops that had to be made for coal and water. Some feared that
the steep inclines in the south of Caithness would be too much for this
new fangled contraption, which confounded its critics by easily
negotiating the Ord and racing to an exhilarating 19 miles an hour on
the straight.

A large crowd greeted the Earl at Wick and the Council made him
an honorary burgess. Next day, in triumph, he set off for Barrogill
Castle (now the Castle of Mey) astonishing all the fit Caithness chiels
that he passed on route.

PEAT

IN these days of rapidly dwindling energy reserves, Caithness
folks can count themselves fortunate in having a fuel supply which
is actually on the increase — peat. So little is being done with this
vast resource of power and chemicals that ere long its usefulness may
be forgotten.

Let us assume that this did happen and speculate upon the
dramatic discovery made by a research scientist in the year 3000
A.D....

In his well-equipped laboratory near Wick, Professor Divot carried
out carefully controlled studies on a thick black organic layer formed
of plant remains whose total decomposition had been prevented
through the exclusion of atmospheric oxygen. This substance was
given the name of PEAT following a "Groat" headline "Pilot
Experiment At Tannach."

The Professor startled the world with his findings: peat could be
cut, dried and used as fuel in homes, factories and power stations.

Some peats could be milled and mixed with the soil thereby
increasing the organic content.

An astonishing variety of products could be derived from peat:
acids, sugars, resins, waxes, adhesives, tannins, etc. The Government was urged to begin immediate exploitation of the PEAT
reserves. (I should point out that Parliament House was at Gillock;
Caithness had long gained its independence from an independent
Scotland but as Wick and Thurso fought over the location of the seat
of Government, a compromise had to be reached.)

No sooner were Divot's findings made public than the environ-
mentalists were up in arms. Their opposition to the utilisation of peat
was total; their platform was highly vocal, their counter-arguments
formidable.

Did Professor Divot not realise that peat workers would be exposed
to poisonous gases released as soon as the peat surface was ruptured?
Had he not considered that in burning hydro-carbons many toxic
substances, including known carcinogens, would be released into the
atmosphere, now mercifully free of the contaminants of earlier
centuries. Surely the acrid peat smoke must be injurious to the lungs.
Moreover, it toughened and aged the skin. And to suggest that such a
dangerous substance should be added to the soil! What untold
damage might it not do to future generations.

Parliament deliberated and voted — No exploitation of PEAT. The
veto was unanimous. The Member for Altnabreac summed up the
feeling of the House: "We have had nuclear power for over 1000 years;
it has served us well and been only a minor health and environmental
hazard. Why disregard this proven system for a fuel source which, if
exploited, could produce risks unknown to man since the 20th
century."

MANANA

A LL too often I am helplessly trapped in the philosophy of
"Don't do today what can be done tomorrow"; this, despite the
fact that the excellent advice "Never put off till tomorrow what you
can do today", was to my knowledge first announced by a peer of the
realm more than two centuries ago.

I suppose that we shall never be able to decide who was the greatest
procrastinator in history. In literature I imagine that Hamlet wins by
a mile, but he put things off in such elegant language that I was
always on his side!

Some psychologists might argue that by putting things off I am
shrinking from a decision, avoiding confrontation and delaying the
moment of truth. This is a grossly unfair analysis. When appearing to
be backsliding or at least dragging my feet there is a reason. The
computer that is my brain has been on a "go-slow" for many years;
which, combined with a second rate programmer, means that instead
of the instant decision, the full out-tray and empty in-tray, all is
loading into the pending compartment to be processed in the brain
box's own time. So, the apparent delaying in making a decision, is
explained on the grounds that all the pros and cons are being

carefully sifted and analysed; the grain sorted out from the chaff; the trivia from the significant .... Francis Drake was quite right to complete his game of bowls on Plymouth Hoe while the Great Armada sailed to England's shores.

Many skilled groups are notorious procrastinators: the cobbler with children whose shoes leak, the plumber with dripping tap, the joiner with squint shelves. Professional groups are no better: doctors don't look after their health; accountants run into debt; worst of all are the lawyers who usually die without leaving a will!

Bureaucracy was founded on the principle of "don't do today what can be done tomorrow", as a governmental safeguard to get the right decision. Within a few years' time we can look forward to a sequence of decision-making that goes from local organisations to Community Councils, Regional Authorities, Devolved Assembly, Westminster and eventually the European Parliament. And so a Belgian might tell an Englishman to tell a Scotsman to tell a Shetlander on Unst where to put his new shed. By then the Shetlanders may have become independent anyway and the decision doesn't matter.

The people of the Highlands have never understood the concern for quick decisions. The Spanish manana implies a delay, a tomorrow, for doing something. In Gaelic there is nothing equivalent for such urgency!

NOSTALGIA

"JANUAR'S blast" fell upon us with sudden violence, the wind as sharp as the barbed hawthorn hedges that march along our lane.

At 1 a.m. on Tuesday a combination of wind, snow and ice had made chaos of our communications and eliminated our power supply. Like many others, we were unaware of being unplugged until the first feet shuffled reluctantly for breakfast.

No power! Och! Maybe it'll be back shortly. But the powerless hours of daylight dragged into the dark folds of night. Candles sprouted their cheer around the room and the peats roared their warmth up the lum. How forlorn the television seemed in its detached silence! Did other households discover long forgotten games and give an all too infrequent airing to conversation?

Our narrow lane, where steeply banked, is a natural receptacle for powdered snow fanned by the wind. By Wednesday vehicles were stranded in this wintry gully until the heroic efforts of a farmer and his tractor restored order.

Wednesday evening. Still no power. But the friendly flames of fire and candle with the help of an oil lamp will suffice for my evening's entertainment — a perusal of Herbert Sinclair's book of "Caithness 1925".

On page eight is a fine study of a Mrs Macphee taken outside Dunbeath Hotel: a round face, watchful, kindly and "full of character .... which, under different circumstances, might have made her somebody."

Following a series of plates of drifters coming in to Wick harbour is a portrait of some gutters where "Highland girls predominate in this view of a yard at Shaltigoe".

Herbert Sinclair met the writer George Bernard Shaw as he was coming out of Thurso post office and took his photograph. Apparently a press representative asked the famous visitor for his impressions of Thurso. "One thousand words for £150", was Shaw's reply!

Five Thurso fishwives with their broad shallow baskets pose pleasantly for the camera.

Not surprisingly the final pictures are of Caithness hoosies. What an agreeable piece of nostalgia on a winter's night!

Maybe the power will be on tomorrow. If not, I can aye burrow cosily into the rich sentiment of the past.

JANUARY DAYS

ALTHOUGH the days have been on the turn a couple of weeks it is only now in early January that the clock seems to have caught up with this calendrical fact. The longest day and shortest day were clearly of significance to man since Stone Age times and even his burial tombs reflect a preoccupation with the subject — it is reputed that if you sit in the chamber of the mound of Maeshowe in Orkney at sunset on the winter solstice, the sun will fleetingly kiss the inner wall of the ancient burial chamber ere it slides behind the horizon.

The sun is now on its slow climb to the June zenith carrying with it the remaining aspirations of New Year resolutions and shedding its watery light on the realities of January.

January is the dispensing month: the food garbage, cans and bottles of Festive indulgence make a welcome exit; the tree, shorn of its needles lies awkwardly by the gate; balloons, tinsel, mistletoe and other seasonal glitter leave walls bare and colourless; Christmas cards are thrown to the children (always retain one as a spare in case you forget to buy one for your wife next year!). January is the reckoning month: you add up all the costs — on second thoughts don't, it might drive you to Old Pulteney! Why do so many bills come in December — with final reminders in January? Governments should legislate to have blanks produced by all computers during the last month of the year.

January is the over-dressed month: No matter what the weather, bairns run around with new toories, scarves and mittens; wifies parade their new boots or stand shivering in the door, feet half over the step to show off their fur-lined slippers; young lassies coyly display shelves of glittering jewellery; embarrassed chiels hide their gaudy ties under gaudier pullovers; owld mannies shuffle past, breathless, in long cravats and polo-necked ganseys. January is the month of dead drapery shops, cleaned out by Christmas crowds. The assistants stare, transfixed, through cold windows or flit, shadowy, 'twixt unruffled coats and dresses. January should be the month for getting buried in books and sharing the gained illumination with friends. It used to be so, not long ago, in Caithness.

January is Burns' month when a great rash of international celebrating will pay homage to the flower of Britain's poets. January is the hopeful month when 20th century man, like his Stone Age predecessors at Maeshowe, has passed through the dark hours of winter and looks, with optimism, to the life-giving sun setting farther and farther in the Northlands.

THE WIRELESS

AS a delayed spring sweeps at speed across the Highlands leaving in its wake the early blooms of the warming sun I give you news that the increased temperature is likely to bring a plague. No, not Asian 'flu, but something far more sinister for which there is (mostly) no known cure — transistors. In rail carriages and buses this bug is known to survive, if in a more soporific state, throughout the winter. In spring, however, it fairly blossoms with batteries recharged, antennae bristling and all tuned up for the long hard summer. It is a bug tolerant of any environment, any altitude. You can find it at 9 a.m. on beaches at Reay, Thurso or Reiss. By 10 o'clock it has spread inland and can be seen in the smallest hamlet, stalking for unwary victims who have failed to plug their ears with cotton wool. It has even been found high up on the slopes of Morven.

During our tropical weather last August I chanced to pay an afternoon visit to Dunnet Sands, one of the most glorious stretches of duneland in all Scotland. What a place to restore the tissues: bracing air, pure as heaven, majestic cliffs, the rhythmic pulse of sea and birds wild and free. But the curative powers of Nature were violated by the strident, shrieking, mindless noise pouring from transistors strategically placed along the shore to ensure that shattered peace was everywhere. As if in some primitive ritual, faces, expressionless, surrounded the black god, in dumb obedience to its screeching utterances. In such circumstances I have a certain sympathy with a gentleman who, on finding a transistor unattended, gave it a solemn and decent burial under three feet of sand. An elderly fellow in Eastbourne was less discreet and hurled an unsuspecting set into the sea. Following prosecution, he informed the magistrate that the fine was money well spent!

Yet, one misses the radio so much when it is out of commission and the modern transistor, when not publicly paraded, is a boon compared to the old wet battery sets. Many readers will remember sitting glued to the faint voice of a commentator getting fainter and fainter as yet another aspiring British hope for the world heavyweight crown had his ambitions knocked senseless under the star spangled banner.

THE PICTS' FIRTH

PETTALAND fjorther (Old Norse for the Pictland or Pentland Firth) has a fairer face this week following the "blowstery" winds of April and early May. The continuous howl of wind from west or south-east can heap up great seas, as Stroma folk found out in 1862 when gigantic waves crashed over the north end of the island, sending sheets of water over the land.

It is a fair possibility that the strait of the Pentland Firth was at one time a river valley that drained into the North Sea Basin; but that was a few million years ago, before Orkney was breached from Caithness.

Now, the restless energy of the oceans is directed at the great flag and sandstone buttresses which slowly yield to the relentless aggression of the sea. Here in the Firth spring tides race at 10 knots and with contrary winds can raise a sea to test the most resolute of ancient mariners.

The races and whirlpools were known to the intrepid Vikings who would have given the widest berths to the Swilkie of Stroma, the Men o' Mey and the Bore of Duncansby. The Vikings did not have the advantage of the Admiralty's publication "North Sea Pilot" which warns: "Before entering the Pentland Firth, all vessels should be prepared to batten down and the hatches of small vessels should be secured even in the finest weather, as the transition from smooth water to a broken sea is so sudden."

Off the old promontory fort on St. John's Head you might see the Men o' Mey in gentle revelry today; come back when the wind is right and watch the demented cavortings of the race where great plumed waves and steaming heads of water hiss and roar.

Off Duncansby Ness the Bore stirs to life on the fast rhythm of the flood running east from the Atlantic. A wind, defying the surging flood, riles him to greatest anger, his long back rising and falling in giant corrugations.

The drumming roll of weighty seas echoes round the geos, fronded by dying waves under the heavy pewter of an angry sky.

> "I must go down to the sea again,
> To the lonely sea and the sky."

If only Masefield had lived on the Caithness coast. What great things it would have done for his poetry!

THE GAMES

"I'M glad that the Games are over," sighed a wifie — and this three weeks after the event! "The Games" are the Halkirk Games; all other Games, being lesser occasions, need a place name added for identification.

On the morning of Saturday, 30th July, anxious eyes scanned the grey sky that blew scubs of rain on to the faces of the kilted and trousered chiels who shuffled about awaiting the band to cheer the spirit en route from the village to the Games field.

A welcoming address by the chieftain, Lord Thurso, and the Games are officially launched. But the Pibroch players have been at their post for nearly two hours and it will be five at night before the dying notes of pipes fade across the greenness of an empty field peppered with the debris of 3000 visitors.

The heavies whet the crowd's appetite with throwing the heavy hammer. Two sturdy locals stagger under the dull weight of a caber nonchalantly tossed by a well-fed chiel from Banchory. The crowd roar their approval.

Lassies, and the occasional loon, go through their elegant footwork on a tartaned platform. Tense relatives and friends hope the judge will pick the right dancer. She never does!

Athletes pound along the track and "whassan" cyclists strain nerve and sinew on one tiring circuit after another.

Thirty lassies sit wi' bonnie bairns and the judge proclaims a winner. You feel sorry for twenty-nine mothers. The bairns don't seem to mind.

At the other end of the field the starter unleashes a horde of peedie boys who stampede towards a tape, half of them claiming that they have won the children's race!

In a park adjoining the Games Field eagle eyes track the clay pigeons and blast them asunder.

The day's events draw to a close. The air is cool and folk are hungry. Bairns want a final trek around the clamouring din of the sideshows. Parents protest and give in.

The pipes play on. Some enthisiasts listen, enthralled.

Alongside a tent a fellow is trying to sleep, overcome by the day's events. There is no awareness in his eyes. A friend gives advice: "Lift yer heid Cheordie and ye'll be all richt!" Cheordie declines. He prefers to leave his head where it is. So will a few others by morning!

In early evening the air has warmed to the stirring pipe marches played in the village. The scene prompts a chiel (thinking of next year) to say: "I wonder if we'll get a good day for The Games?"

HOLIDAYMAKERS

IT is high noon on Saturday and the sun has been beating down for hours on the Costa del Braal, Halkirk. Similar weather, I believe, has been forecast for the Reay Riviera, the Golden Mile of Dunnet and the Lido (harbour) of Lybster where young loons learned to swim under the lee of herring-scented boats. The village's picturesque harbour has become quite a mecca for tourists (I met a fellow from Dunbeath there last month) and sleek fibre-glass coaches are now a common sight on the quay. The visitors frequently ask for toilet facilities and we in turn point vaguely to a near horizon studded with knee deep heather, but seldom do the stressed tourists take advantage of Nature's outdoor amenities. Perhaps by next summer we shall be able to supply facilities acceptable to urban modesty.

Recently we overheard complaints from some visitors that there was so little to do up here: no night clubs, no rows of gaming machines, no streets of flashing neon lights "to cheer the place up", and no central bingo-orientated complex at which disciples might gather to alleviate the tedium of their Northern holiday.

On reflection I have wondered if we could persuade the Hospital Board to consider the appointment of a medical practitioner who has specialised in the treatment of bored tourists to sit in Wick market square in an office lined with one armed bandits and gaudy lights waltzing across the frontage of his door. Particularly bad cases could be shipped on the m.v "Social Security" to Stroma (although a choppy crossing it avoids the lengthy journey to Spain) where the island would have been transformed into a haven for tourists, its illuminations eclipsing the grossest vulgarities of Blackpool.

If properly marketed the Stroma centre could attract a colossal overseas clientele and obtain much needed foreign currency to repay the International Monetary Fund the vast sums that we have borrowed to help the Government whose expenditure is so high because of the large number of cases that have to be treated in SMART (Stroma's Medical Arcade for Restive Tourists).

Hush .... I hear the roar of an exhaust as a burnished coach swings over the bridge into the village. Forty tourists from Germany alight waving their proud Deutchmarks while uttering astonished cries at the cheap prices in the shops and making favourable noises about the weather on the Costa del Braal.

NATURE AND POLITICIANS

IS this the eclipse of summer? The TV weather charts show sequences of fronts moving in rapidly across the Atlantic, the closely set isobars signalling strong winds with rain showers.

The bird choirs seem more muted too. The joyous full-throated song of high summer has given way to less exuberant music: it is more of a mechanical playing, not so melodious nor so inspiring. When the birds are less in evidence the insects take the musical stage, especially the "murmur of innumerable bees".

One bird very much on the stage at this time of year is the grouse, the prince of British game. There'll be little peace for the poor souls now as the tweeded armies march across the moors to the harsh barking of the guns.

Over the grouse moors snake the pylons of the North of Scotland Hydro Electric Board which was founded by Act of Parliament forty years ago. The man given most credit for this achievement was a Scot of remarkable talent and foresight, Tom Johnston, journalist, politician and (arguably) our last great Secretary of State.

As it is some ten years ago since the last of the Board's stations was commissioned it is encouraging to see a proposal by them to construct two small dams and power stations on the south shore of Loch Maree in Wester Ross. Perhaps Caithness has little water power potential on its land mass, but it has enormous generating capacity lying dormant in the strong tides of the Pentland Firth. Power from peat, the atom and the sea will all "fuel" my argument of independence for Caithness, with all incomers paying a handsome tax to live in this civilised land so that locals can maintain a high standard of living. It all seems so logical to me. I cannot think of a single rational argument against it. Can you?

While on the theme of rational thoughts, or the lack of them, I was lately confronted by a brisk lady with tightly-coiffured hair crowned by an elegant blue hat. She looked the type who would breeze in your front door, uninvited, esconse herself in your favourite chair and then, having swept a professional eye along your bookshelves, enquire why you had not provided your offspring with a set of Blipp's Encyclopaedias. I was entirely wrong. She had the honourable and demanding occupation of housewife but had dolled herself up for the county show, which she chose as a political background.

"I resent a male chauvinist like you always attacking Mrs Thatcher. She does the work of two men!"

— Laurel and Hardy?

ROBBIE BURNS

S OME autumns ago we drove past Ellisland farm, a pleasant pastoral setting to the north of Dumfries. When Robbie Burns farmed here the land was badly drained, in weak heart and unfenced. In many respects Ellisland was in poorer condition than the farms which Robbie and his father had valiantly struggled with in Ayrshire. There was not even a house on Ellisland and his family had to live in a damp squalid hut until a house was built.

"I'm dwindled down to mere existence."

Yet, in spite of the appalling wretchedness of their living conditions and the gruelling uphill struggle ahead of him the poet was not downcast. While sitting over the smoking embers of the hut fire he composed one of his most tender love songs.

"Of a' the airts the wind can blaw."

Poor Robbie had problems with the tradesmen; they were far behind schedule in house construction and many urgent appeals had to be made to them. To compound his worries, the weather was foul, the harvest almost disastrous and "I am scarce able to hold up my head with this fashionable influenza".

It is just as well that by this time Burns had acquired his excise post which he was later to call "my sheet anchor in life". Ellisland, he wrote, "is in the last stage of worn-out poverty" and "all my surplus had to go .... to a younger brother and three sisters in Ayrshire".

Outwith house, farm, health and various financial problems Robbie and wife Jean took in the family of his uncle who had died suddenly while still a young man. Into the Ellisland home also came Robbie's younger brother who seemed unable to settle into any job.

Burns' excise duties were considerable, as, in the latter half of the 18th century the tax was levied on items such as alcohol, coffee, various juices, malt, hides and skins, soap, building materials, salt, sweets, tobacco, snuff, etc. As the duty on these items was charged during the manufacture, excisemen had to make frequent calls on premises at all hours of the day and night. In fact Burns, in the course of his duties, travelled some 200 miles a week on a horse which he had to provide out of his own pocket!

There is an abundance of evidence to show that Burns was both a conscientious and efficient employee who maintained meticulous records and wrote careful reports to his employers.

His government post could, at times, bring him into conflict with his own political views, such as his opinions on the American Revolution and his obvious sympathy for the French Revolution.

So, the picture we have of Burns at Ellisland, is of a mature family man, grossly overworked, taking on family and financial commitments that drained his meagre resources. Between the farm work and his excise job convivial social evenings in Dumfries must have been few.

It is regrettable that a narrow-minded teetotaller was the poet's first biographer, a man who would have had about as much camaraderie towards Burns as Hitler to the Kremlin.

A FISHY TALE

JUST at the tail end of the fishing season a chiel in Sutherland was trying to sell me a salmon. He had happened to land it trying to catch trout. Such is the misfortune of some anglers!

"You shouldn't be selling fish caught illegally", said I, not really caring one whit. "It's part of the black economy. Mrs Thatcher, among others, would thoroughly disapprove".

Within minutes we were exploring the black economy and considering some of the elements in it: being employed and accepting dole money or social security payments; money earned but not declared for tax purposes; payment in kind; a worker taking a tool from a factory; a clerk a pen from his office; a travelling salesman who submits false costs claims; a squatter who pays no rent, etc., etc.

By far the most major component in this black economy is the tax dodger. He skins far more from society than the much maligned social security scroungers, who are now hounded by officials, thus gaining a small economic return for the national outlay. A much greater financial success rate could be achieved if Government appointed officials turned their attention to, for example, proceeds from one-armed bandits.

Yet, I suspect, to the vast majority of us evading tax is a kind of game, and a very lucrative one for some members of the business world. But it is a crime. Theft on a large scale!

It is one of the truisms of capitalist society that people earning the most handsome incomes gain the greatest perks: company cars, free continental holidays and paid meals. If such happenings are fair game for the few geese then officialdom shouldn't quibble when all the ganders try to get in on the act!

The hotel and catering trade is renowned in legend if not in fact for its well organised black economy. A hotelier in Grampian informed me of a kitchen employee who confessed to taking "about 10 dozen eggs a week for five years." The owner of a small hostelry in Inverness discovered that his barman was taking in his own bottles of whisky and selling these by the nip. What an excellent example of private enterprise! How do you reduce such activities in the licensed and catering trade? Would paying the employees a higher income help?

The black economy appears to be highly developed in Russia, where even in the state-owned stores sales staff will keep the best goods for the customers who are willing to pay a premium.

The black economy then seems common to all political systems .... how regrettable it is .... but I did enjoy the salmon.

THREE BOOKS

T HREE welcome books fell bounteously upon me at Xmas: 'Dogs' by various children, 'Highland Pack' by Neil Gunn, and 'My Life with Nye' by Jennie Lee.

The first of these was gleefully presented to me by two cronies with obvious tongue in cheek, as I have recently had a dog thrust upon me; or, from a canine point of view I have been inflicted upon it. I sat reading 'Highland Pack' to the appropriate music of the Wallochmore Ceilidh Band's latest recording — the gift of a Member of the Halkirk Parliament. 'Highland Pack' is the ideal book for somebody who is frequently interrupted as it consists of a collection of essays on country life, many of which appeared in the Scots Magazine during the early years of the last war. Mostly they are concerned with the day to day happenings around a farmhouse, but occasionally include excursions to remote places, expecially in the Hebrides. In the book, time drifts somewhat uncertainly through the sting of winter, the expectancy of April, the burnishing of summer and the fulfilment of autumn. It is an oddment of writings, as the author explains, gathered in the manner of the wandering pack man. Yet every item in the pack is worthy of purchase: Each a splendidly tailored garment whether of the frightened grouse chick on the moor, or the galloping hare, the lonely curlew, the wild woodlands, bounding streams or the awesome wonder of the heavens. Marvellous stuff to be set aside and taken from the shelf again in our next cold spell.

Still, at least the conclusion of Neil Gunn's book took me to 'My Life with Nye', and at the outset I must declare an interest and an obvious prejudice: Nye Bevan was the great hero of my teenage years: Nye, the 14-year-old boy with the stammer who went down the coal pits and later educated his brilliantly receptive mind so that he was the welcome poet, philospher and internationalist of some of the most outstanding intellects in the country. He was also a man of strong physique and enormous vitality who worked with a ferocious appetite. He robustly articulated his political faith and frequently held the Commons spellbound with his marvellous oratory.

He was, too, a man of vision who feared the consequences of allowing Russia and America to carve up the world between them. His political philosophy was democratic socialism, a philosophy based on the firm conviction that "free men can use free institutions to solve the social and economic problems of the day, if they are given a chance to do so."

In the post-war Cabinet Bevan often had unyielding opposition from Gaitskill who had the block vote of the right wing unions on his side. (The block vote was as contemptible then as now, but how many right wingers complained about it?) Even in Opposition the right wing of the party was hostile towards him but its venom was less poisonous than that of the scorpions of the Tory press.

On a bleak December day in 1959 Nye Bevan went into hospital. Seven months later he was dead, struck down in the prime of his powers. On the 5th July 1960 the radio announced his death. It was one of the most emotional moments of my life.

HOLIDAY THOUGHTS

T HE land is glistening, the air is flinty and hits the lungs with eye-watering impact; you don't need pep pills to face the day after a few whiffs of this Arctic wind!

Children, pallid faces pinched with cold, shuffle to school with hunched, reluctant gait. A billy-goat turns a baleful eye on his harsh, white world, aggression numbed and mind unaware that some of our

Brothers have hastily dispensed with the festive cheer and now, in customary comradely spirit, prepare us for the winter of their discontent:

> Blow, blow, thou winter wind,
> Thou art not so unkind
> As man's ingratitude.

Rooks skip about the blanketed fields, scrape away the snow and stab the rock-hard ground in a frantic search for food, their guttural voices stilled by the gripping frosts. The dull, dry hawthorn hedge offers little shelter from piercing winds. Nor does the open latticework of trees, two-dimensional against a bare sky hung with metallic stars.

This is indoor weather! This is the time for clookin' over a roaring log fire. Anonymous, lifeless electric fires offer no compensation against the blasts; they merely warm the body but fail to cheer the mind.

Some television programmes attempt to cheer. For instance the benign, agreeable Cliff Michelmore wishes to transport me to other worlds with his weekly holiday stint. Sun-drenched tourists lie cheek by jowl on sandy beaches; the less brave (or more sensible) perch under shady umbrellas sipping their gins and tonics. There is a large queue at a shop bearing the sign "Genuine English Food. Fish and Chips." in the cool of the evening there are night clubs and Spanish dancers. Accommodation is in a 20-storey hotel. The Sunday press pursues the holiday theme. "Forget it's winter: Book two weeks in the sun. You can be packaged for £195."

I dislike being packaged by either press, radio or television. Nor can I forget it is winter, but I have introduced brief rays of warmth into the village by borrowing a crony's sun lamp. By the middle of February I shall have a tan that would fool Enoch Powell. This will set me up for the summer and an exclusive unpackaged holiday on the peaceful Costa del Braal, Halkirk.

Beyond Caithness

ORKNEY'S NORTH ISLES

"Back again? It's the time o' year o' it." A familiar, lilting Orcadian voice greeted me as I landed in the northern green isles in my usual summer pilgrimage by way of British Airways (Wick-Kirkwall) and Loganair on to the island of Stronsay, giving a total flying time of 23 minutes. Although more than twice the cost of the sea journey, many travellers deem it worthwhile.

For two idyllic weeks I can avoid a telephone and writing letters, jettison the tie and miss a day or two's contact with the razor. I have not read a newspaper or heard a news bulletin in the past week and I don't suppose the world is any the worse for it. Surely it will survive another week without my taking an interest in its political and economic ills?

Normally a poor sleeper, here I manage 10 hours on the trot, struggling to life to consume coffee and toast which is hastily followed by "dinner" at 11 a.m. Piece time at 2.30 is almost another meal, followed by a substantial tea at 5 o'clock. A cooked supper at 10 p.m. is not uncommon; four meals in eleven hours is most demanding and the only way to prepare the gastric juices for this intake is to plowter in the silage pit, heave hay bales, or wend one's way round the cliffed headlands lonely in an Orkney sea. Here, free as the gliding fulmars, the mind soars on its flights of wild fancy, way, way across the sea of the Northmen to sagas of the past. A skraiking scorrie sunders the reverie and sets the feet homeward.

Homeward to another feed and preparation for the island barn dance to fine Scottish music and home brew to quench the thirst. The barn is a sea of contented faces as befits the men and families of the land and sea—men as adjusted to their environment as they are to life itself. Their progress is a progress of efficiency, not the complication of simplicity which seems to bedevil so much of today's change.

Perhaps our decision makers might reflect on the words of Thor

Heyerdahl: "Without the farmer and the fisherman modern society would collapse, with all its shops, and all its pipes and wires. The farmers and fishermen represent the nobility of modern society, who share their crumbs with the rest of us who run about with papers and screwdrivers attempting to build a better world without a blueprint."

UP TO SHETLAND

Banks of heavy pewter cloud loitered about the grey coast of Caithness. It was clear over Duncansby Head and from Loganair you gazed down on the great geos slashed in the headlands. To the west the Merry Men o' Mey cavorted wildly near the laboured ploughing of a cargo boat.

Over South Ronaldsay Loganair Captain Andy Alsop pointed out young grey seals lying in the shelter of two steep-walled inlets. (Are breeding colonies of these seals being noted and recorded in Caithness?)

The British Airways plane from Kirkwall to Shetland is late; the incoming flight was delayed as somebody, somewhere, was on strike. Eventually away and over the fertile green fields of Orkney, past the rock walls of Fair Isle, towards looming Sumburgh Head. At the airport are eight helicopters and three aeroplanes. Dozens of people jostle in the lounge and hopeful taxi drivers wait to whisk you 30 miles to Lerwick.

North of the town's harbour is one extensive development after another; new concrete buildings going up, stone houses coming down; big cranes and peerie cranes; bulldozers and forklifts; boats of all sizes and the weirdest of shapes. Pyramids of coated pipes make artistic shapes and patterns in the setting sun.

The shops are crowded and the tills jingle incessantly. Somehow it all seems incongruous that in a small shop in these Northern Isles the soft cadences of the Shetlander are drowned in a cosmopolitan caucus and it in turn abruptly shattered by the strident, petulant tones of a pukka Sahib complaining that some of his ordered goods had not arrived. A remarkably patient assistant offers apologetic explanations. To no avail.

Soon the thick oil will course along its submarine veins and pump on to the ancient shores of Shetland, where by the long voe of Sullom the gluttonous tanks will take their fill and lie gorged in the twilights of a Viking land.

The black liquid gold is a great magnet drawing sturdy men from the harvests of the land and sea that have nourished Shetlanders for

over a thousand generations. Maybe they will return again when the
last dying soughs echo from the wells in the heartland of the North
Sea. Perhaps the dead rigs on the broad brows of land will once more
grow fields of fulsome grain; and contented faces empty nets heavy
with silver darlings, for their cherished Land o' the Simmer Dim.

DORNOCH

Even Dornoch can look dreich on a day like this: a heavy grey
sky, stinging east wind and sudden scubs of rain.

The cathedral retains its solid dignity despite the capricious elements. It is 760 years since the bishopric was moved here from
Halkirk after the lawless folk in that area had burned their unloved
prelate.

That was not, however, the first religious connection that Caithness had with Dornoch. Centuries earlier the bringer of the Christian
message to Dornoch was reputedly St. Finbarr, possibly a native of
Caithness, who had attended the great Ninian's centre of learning at
Candida Casa in Galloway.

There is no firm written evidence of St. Finbarr's activities in
Dornoch but his name is still alive in local legend. Moreover, the old
Celtic church, named Templebar in his honour, survived until the
17th century. St. Barr's Fair, one of the highlights of the local
calendar, continued until the early 1900s. A little farther along the
coast, at Embo, new fishing nets were blessed in the name of Barr.

Early missionary activity is likely to have been patchy and it was
probably long after Finbarr's time before the Northern Picts were
Christianised.

In the latter part of the 8th century the earliest marauding and
colonising Vikings assailed our shores. One of the memorable battles
of their later activities took place near Embo. The Vikings had landed
at Little Ferry where they were seen by Sir Richard de Moravia from
his castle at Skelbo.

He received a message from the Earl of Sutherland to attack and
despite his small force he attacked the enemy. In the meantime the
Earl gathered all able-bodied men and hastened to Richard's aid.
Most of the Vikings were killed. The Earl engaged the Viking chief in
personal combat, became disarmed and picked up the severed leg of a
horse with which he killed the chief. And that is why Dornoch has the
heraldic horse's shoe on its coat of arms. Unfortunately, the brave Sir
Richard de Moravia was killed in the encounter and later buried in
Dornoch Cathedral which was put to fire in the 16th century when

the Mackays descended on Dornoch to attack the Murrays. Needless
to say Caithness folk were also involved in that sad skirmish!

GEORGEMAS TO TAIN

It is a "moochy" day for joining the southbound train at busy
Georgemas Junction. The ponderous diesel charges away. No
passengers at Scotscalder and a dearth of them at Altnabreac too.
Forsinard and Kinbrace also drew a blank. I am highly honoured: the
only chiel British Rail uplifted between Wick and Helmsdale!

The sky is still heavy, with occasional canals of light from the
winter sun cutting through the grey cloud to spill brightness on the
claret moor. Deer stalk the land in search of better grazing and a
hungry kestrel rakes the ground with binocular vision. Life on the
hill is becoming hard as the talons of winter grip tighter.

The train pauses a while at Brora, then sneaks off quietly for
Golspie, passing Dunrobin on the way. Here the Duke of Sutherland
built himself a private station and even ordered the railway company
to push on laying the track northwards before the necessary Act had
been passed by Parliament! Such was the power of Dukes. Sitting
atop Ben Bhraggie is the statue of the first Duke, "erected by a
grateful tenantry." What a commanding view he has across the
Moray Firth.

From the Mound to Ardgay the train loops inland following the
Duke's wishes to have rail access to the interior sheeplands and the
great sales at Rogart and Lairg, the heart of Sutherland's roads
system.

At the Mound is the causeway, built by Telford, which almost cuts
off Strath Fleet, an area largely filled in with sediment and now one
of the best alder swamps in Britain. William Young, who with
Patrick Sellar ran the Sutherland estate for a period in the early 19th
century, wanted to drain Loch Fleet and create vast farms. Young
had no consideration for other people's money and wasted huge sums
on the enormous Sutherland estate which, at 1⅓ million acres, was
one of the biggest in Europe.

The train accelerates down the treeclad slopes of the Shin valley,
where the larches have shed their winter coats, their new garb a dull
brown amid the evergreens. Lairg, Shin, Cannich, Fannich, Inver-
moriston are names associated with schooldays when so many men
from the village had to move south to seek work in lands beyond the
Ord.

Culrain to Invershin. Is this the shortest distance between two
railway stations still in operation in Great Britain?

Tain! The heavens have opened again and great pools of water have gathered in the fields. On one occasion some years ago high tides, strong winds and heavy rain coincided to maroon some golfers in the local club house. Anxiously the police contacted them by phone to find out if all was well. "No hurry for a rescue," said a cheery voice, "I have the key to the bar!"

TO THE UISTS

Monday: What a lovely day to drive to Ullapool! The gentlest of breezes, clear sky and a warm sun. This lengthy jagged coastline of the western highlands has little economic wealth on land but an abundance of riches under the sea. As far back as the 16th century boats, under sail, were fishing commercially for herring and Lochbroom was already well-known for its catches of the "silver darlings". The herring were salted on nearby Tanera island before being shipped to markets in the south. Although the trade potential in cured fish was all too evident, some 200 years were to elapse before the British Fisheries Society was formed to develop harbours such as Pulteneytown, Tobermory, Mallaig and Ullapool.

It is midday and the Suilven is about to sail to Ullapool. Lochbroom and the Minch are deceptively calm. Will it be so on Saturday?

Stornoway is one of the great natural harbours of Britain, flanked by protruding headlands including Arnish point, the site of Lewis Offshore Limited, where workers are building barges and other structures for the oil industry.

We drive up a narrow road to the crofting settlement of Gress where I am handsomely entertained by a Caithness crony and his good wife.

Tuesday: One of the officials I meet in the education office informs me his wife is a Wicker! What an auspicious start to the day! At Radio Nan Eilean we discuss the possibility of lectures in Gaelic and English. Alas! I have problems aplenty with the latter without attempting to crack the linguistic complexities of the former.

Wednesday : The wind has whipped up from the south-west and low cloud draws a depressing veil across the landscape. The Loganair pilot informs us he'll fly to Benbecula down the coast. "Put on the headphones", he exclaims, "and we'll examine the geology". I'd much rather shut my eyes and pray but effect an interest until a descending torrent of air sweeps the plane seawards giving the passengers great cracks on the head in the process. My liking for terra firma is strengthened.

What a wilderness of land and water in the Uists; it is almost as if the good Lord could not decide what to do with this ancient landmass.

Thursday and Friday: Visits by cars to North Uist and South Uist, reaching the extremity of the island to take photographs of Eriskay and Barra, two Hebridean islands where I have yet to venture.

Saturday: The boat leaves at 8 a.m. from Stornoway escorted by a solitary gannet, who finding no suitable scraps from crew or passengers wheels away for the Lewis coast. Near the Summer Isles in Lochbroom a score of gannets suddenly appear and wing their elegant way around us.

The road to the north is quiet. I drive slowly through Bonar Bridge. It will be strange passing through that pleasant village now with no Willie Sinclair to visit. What a great ambassador he was for Caithness and Scotland. Everyone who met him was the better for the warmth of his words and the richness of his humour. He was never dull, never complaining, but aye interesting and constantly refreshing. The mid 80's seems all too short a life span for men of his calibre.

BY LOCH DUICH

I have passed the five sisters of Kintail on many occasions yet have only taken one photograph of them, such are the vagaries of the weather in the West Highlands. When the heavy veils of mist are cast aside, when the peaks rise against the azure sky and the sun spreads its golden warmth on the ancient summits, you are looking at one of the glories of Scottish scenery.

The mountains, now part of the National Trust's empire, were at one time the proud property of the McKenzies of Kintail, when, according to legend, they were given their name.

The story has it that in days gone by a man who dwelt by the shores of Loch Duich had seven daughters each of remarkable beauty with characters beyond reproach. Not surprisingly, their thoughts ultimately turned to the subject of young men and they yearned for the day when they might meet some suitable companions. They did not have too long to wait . . . .

Following a severe westerly gale a broken ship sailed into Loch Duich's long sheltered arm of the sea. The vessel eventually lowered its anchor and despatched a small rowing boat towards the shore. To the pleasant surprise of the seven sisters the craft was oared by two handsome young fellows whom they invited to come and meet their father.

Being a Highlander of customary generous disposition he asked the young men to stay at his household until their ship departed. They readily agreed and within days had acquired eyes for two of the sisters whom they asked to join ship as their brides. The father consented, but encountered fierce opposition from his other daughters who were upset at the thought of their sisters' departure.

The diplomatic brothers intervened in the dispute to say that they had five handsome brothers back in Ireland! They suggested that in return for the hands of the two sisters they would send their five brothers to Loch Duich. Alas! The five brothers never materialised!

The father, fearing that his five daughters would soon lose their beauty sought the advice of a local wizard, who informed the girls that he had a plan that would make them permanently beautiful. The girls were thrilled and eagerly awaited the wizard's spell. Soon his magic was completed and the girls were transformed into the five sisters of Kintail whose unfading beauty will allure lovers till the end of time.

A NORTHERN WEEK

Monday: It is a dour day yielding nothing to the sun over the relaxing peace of the Causewaymire. From a rise near Latheron the eye falls on an incongruous monster set against the horizon: the giant legs of an oil rig stride towards the Inner Firth.

Many people find the A9 a dull road. I never tire of it, finding something new on each journey in these strange lands south of the Ord.

On to Inverness and meetings at 2, 4.30 and 7 o'clock. Three successful deliberations in one day; how satisfying in our age when committees proliferate to delay decision-making!

Tuesday: There is a flood of brightness over the fertile Laich o'Moray and the rolling farmlands of Buchan. The Granite City bristles in the distance, its sturdy stone buildings dwarfed by the stark ugliness of functional concrete structures. What an appalling architectural heritage we are leaving to future generations!

Wednesday: It is a raw day in Inverness and the bookshop's bright beacon is welcoming. Inside you scan the serried ranks of tome after tome on Scotland. It is encouraging to see this upsurge of interest in our landscape, heritage and culture. It is a savage indictment of our educational and political system that generations of pupils were turned out of school with so little knowledge of their Nation's past.

On to Strathpeffer to blether. The village was a bustling place in Victorian times as trainloads of hypochondriacs with too much in their pockets and too little in their heads sampled the sulphur waters of the tiny spa.

Thursday: By a sharp bend near Drumnadrochit a wild cat bounds on to the road, bares its teeth at the on-rushing car and vanishes into a thicket. The long ribbon of Loch Ness is the colour of mercury. No monster stirs its surface. The road is too quiet. Nearly all the tourists have gone to roost.

At Invergarry I meet a friendly couple who plan to move up to Caithness. They fell for the great expanses of sky, the wild coastline, sparkling fresh air and the warmth of the people.

Friday: Great plumes of smoke herald Fort William, dominated by the Ben, dusted in snow. In the town's West Highland Museum is a section devoted to paraphernalia of Prince Charles. I have no enthusiasm for the fellow, regarding him as one of the greatest tragedies to afflict the Highlands.

On to Lochailort Castle. What a remarkable evening: a calm, crisp air, with millions of stars in a flawless sky and timeless hills lording the valley.

Saturday: Freezing fog and a skin of ice on the road. Trundling lorries laden with pulp-mill timber heave out of the misty swirl. On the east coast the last wisps of fog are melting under the low sun and the green grass of the fields is singing softly in the orange tints of winter warmth.

PICTS

I was following the roads and the miles to Dundee last weekend attending a conference on "The Picts". Suitably Pictified I departed three days later leaving litter-strewn streets to hug the coast to Aberdeen, past the fields of broken barley.

The leaves of autumn have begun their earthward journey, their gold gently scattered about the sodden land. The distant hills are broken flints against the morning haze.

Inverness gets busier by the week. It is a relief to escape the noise and pressure of folk and look across the Firth to the broad fertile tongue of the Black Isle. The green acres of Easter Ross give way to more grudging land as the train cuts inland to Lairg, the nerve centre of Sutherland's road system. The all pervasive bracken is around us, its spread, I am told, resulting from the rapid change of a cattle to sheep economy during the 19th century's age of improvements.

Near Kildonan the young conifers run their boring way up heathered hills. An American tourist leans out of the window to take a picture of the land of his forefathers. He shakes his head sadly at the mute field clearance cairns, lifeless between the rushing ribbons of rail and road.

The train escapes the confines of the valleys to thread its way across the far flung moors. We've come to Caithness.

"I rather like wild natural landscape", observed the American. You could, of course, debate endlessly on how our landscapes would have looked if man and his animals had not exploited them. Much of the natural wildernesses of the North Highlands that some conservationists rave about have only been "natural" for the past few centuries following man's depredations. Thinking of conservation brings me back to the Dundee conference and its excursions to visit sites of earthhouses, old churches and symbol stones that have been maintained for our enlightment and education. Most instructive are the ancient slabs on which the Pictish sculptor-artists carved with such consummate skill their elegant vigorous animals and enigmatic abstract designs.

MULL AND IONA

A south-westerly wind has blown unceasingly for three days and white crested waves hurry through the Sound of Iona. There seems to be some doubt if the ferry will make any more crossings. My companions have already made up their minds — we go tomorrow.

The weather gods are kinder the next day and we're off from Fionnphort in Mull to the hamlet of Baile Mor, which lies in a fertile strip of soil developed on the ancient Torridonian sandstone of east Iona. Although there is evidence of settlement in Iona from ancient times, one of the earliest known descriptions of the island comes from the English historian Bede writing about the year 730AD. The name used by Bede is Hii insula, whereas Columba's biographer Adomnan called it Ioua. So it would seem that the modern name resulted from the mistranslation of an early manuscript with an N replacing the U to give Iona.

One can hardly think of the name Iona without linking it to that of St Columba who came to the small island with twelve monastic companions in 563 from Dal Riata in Northern Ireland. Most of our knowledge of the saint comes from the Abbot Adomnan writing about 100 years after Columba died. The buildings of the Columban mission would have been mostly of timber and so it is no surprise that nothing of them remains. However, traces of a substantial earthwork that outlined the monastic site are still clearly visible, particularly to the west of the road. Within this penisula there would have been a small church, living quarters (cells) for Columba and the monks and a variety of buildings including a scriptorium where the highly important work of copying manuscripts was carried out.

In the century following Columba's death the abbey on Iona continued to flourish, with off-shoot monasteries being founded in North Ireland, Southern Scotland (Old Melrose) and Northern England (Lindisfarne).

At Iona it would seem that Columba had placed much emphasis on writing, particularly in copying the scriptures. Many scholars now think that the glorious illuminated gospel work "The Book of Kells" has more in common with 8th century Pictish sculpture and the beautifully executed stone crosses on Iona and Islay. An origin in Iona seems a distinct possibility.

The great religious and cultural centre of Iona was struck by the Viking whirlwind in 798. With the arrival of the Norsemen Iona's remote and exposed position was vulnerable to attack. Successive Viking raids in the early 9th century drove the monks back to Northern Ireland, the root area of Iona's inspiration.

STIRLING
AND BANNOCKBURN

A low'rin sky hangs over us spilling endless rain.

At a garage near Stirling I complain to the attendant: "What weather you have here!" Without replying, he eyes me stonily. "You're from Caithness. That's where the rain is made and exported!"

"That's typical of our generosity," says I, "not keeping all the good things of life to ourselves!"

On to Stirling. What a remarkable resemblance there is between the town, its dominant castle, and Scotland's capital. The original Stirling Castle would have been mainly constructed of wooden buildings and palisades. But by the time of Bannockburn the original had long since gone and what the visitors see today dates mainly from the 15th century.

One of the most important buildings is the Great Hall which was ruthlessly altered at the end of the 18th century to leave an empty shell where a sumptuous building once stood. Workmen were busy restoring the building to its former eminence, a task that will probably take them into next century. The adjacent palace built by James V in the 16th century is of immense architectural interest. The exterior has a variety of carved heads, small statues and grotesque animal gargoyles.

The chapel Royal, built by King James VI, was later appropriated by the military as an armoury. New ceilings and floors were introduced, the latter of Caithness flagstones. These have gone except for a few at the entrance doorway which contrast starkly with the cobbled courtyard.

On to Bannockburn, where the Scots triumphed over the Auld Enemy on 24th June, 1314. Stirling Castle was delivered by the English to Bruce who destroyed the fortifications. The new visitors' centre at Bannockburn, with its audio-visual room does much to improve the perception of the battle.

Despite the torrential rain we go in solemn procession to Bruce's statue, while our English crony takes the dog for a walk!

Bannockburn! Such an unpoetic name for the site that ensured a nation's survival. What a pathetic lot the Scots of the 20th century are compared to those who followed Wallace and Bruce. How many of us, I wonder, still stir to Bruce's ringing Declaration of Arbroath (1320).

"For we fight not for glory, nor riches, nor honours, but for freedom alone, which no good man gives up except with his life."